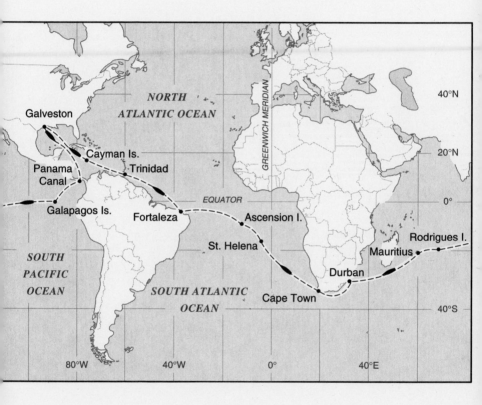

The Oceans Are Waiting

The
Oceans
Are Waiting

Around the World on the Yacht TIGGER

SHARON RAGLE

Sheridan House

First published 2002 by
Sheridan House Inc.
145 Palisade Street
Dobbs Ferry, NY 10522

Library of Congress Cataloging-in-Publication Data

Ragle, Sharon
  The oceans are waiting: around the world on the
  Yacht Tigger / Sharon Ragle.
      p. cm.
  ISBN 1-57409-145-X (hardcover: alk. paper)
  1.Tigger (Yacht) 2. Ragle, Sharon-Journeys.
  3.Voyages around the world. I. Title.

  G440.T56R34 2002
  910.4'1-dc21   2002011394

Printed in the United States of America

ISBN 1-57409-145-X

Text design by Keata Brewer

Contents

Acknowledgments

To my dear friends and sisters-of-my-heart, Kate Evans and Elaine Vogel, I send my most heartfelt thanks and love. Without you—each in your own separate way—planting the seed of this new adventure, I would not have been brave enough, or felt free enough to attempt to put pen to paper (or fingers to keyboard).

When the first clumsy draft was done, it was Jerry Miller who said, "This could possibly be publishable!" Then Ted Black read it and said the same thing. I was on a roll! Thanks to both of you for your encouraging words.

Brenda Gatlin, my daughter-in-law, spent hour upon hour proofing and polishing and without her efforts, I'm sure it would still be in some publisher's slush pile. You are wonderful Brenda, and you have my love and thanks.

My thanks to Paul Mirto, map maker extraordinaire, for the fine route map.

And thank you, Lothar Simon. You gave me a chance, and in your gracious way, guided this novice, and kept my anxiety and neuroses at a reasonable level!

For Dave—my husband and best friend—
I'm still amazed at the miracle.

The Oceans Are Waiting

1

The Beginning of a Dream

My fortune cookie said, "Great adventures await those willing to turn the corner." When I read those words, I got a chill. I just knew something was up. Not that I am an especially strong believer in destiny. Just the opposite. That kind of experience has always seemed far beyond me; that was for bigger lives than mine. So imagine my surprise. Destiny was about to take me by the hand. And whether it was to gently nudge me in a certain direction or shake me until I cried, I already sensed that when destiny called, there was no turning back.

At the time I was single, having divorced many years earlier and raised my two daughters and a son as a single parent. One marriage was enough for me. It had left me sad and very skeptical, both of marriage in general and myself and marriage in particular. So I was content to be alone, go my way with my children, and have a man friend here and there. I liked men, just not men and marriage. I preferred to stay safe and single.

Then one day my whole world changed—just like that. The children were adults and on their own. I was out on business in West Texas at the time, driving down the freeway on the vast, flat prairie. My eyes were on the road and my mind on nothing in particular, when out of nowhere, a voice said to me, "You are going to buy a boat and sail around the world." Before I could even think, "Where did *that* come from?" another part of me just said, "Yes," and my fate was sealed. Whose voice was it? I don't know, but it was a voice of authority, and it was as if each cell in my body joined my spirit and just breathed, "Yes," in unison.

All these years later, I can honestly report I've never again had that experience, although there are plenty of times when I've wished I would. That perfect voice takes away all decision making. There's no waffling. No wondering whether I should do this or do that. The only decision I had to make was how to do it, not if I should do it. The big question—what to do with the rest of my life—was gone. Now it was a series of little problems to solve. For an anxious person like me this was a godsend. Of course now, years later, mission accomplished, I'm back to, "What to do with the rest of my life." I'd really like to hear that voice again.

Let me be very clear here—I'm no kook. At least I wasn't before the voice came into my life and gave me this very strange mission. And I don't think it was God, although I can't think of anyone else it might have been. No wait, I suppose I do think it was God, even if that sounds far-fetched and much too arrogant. I won't try to convince you one way or the other. If someone had told me this story, I would have wondered what kind of interesting pills they were taking. I'll leave you to draw your own conclusions, but trust me, that's the way it happened.

In some ways I suppose I was predisposed to hear this kind of command; being someone who had always been a dreamer. Years ago, as a teen in Seattle, I would imagine myself on a South Sea Island. I would stand on the bluff near our house overlooking Puget Sound and watch the ships leave port to make their way out to the Pacific Ocean and wonder where they were going. In those days you could read the daily paper and find out what ships were leaving and where they were going. Pago Pago in particular conjured up images of adventure and derring-do. I would see myself standing on the deck of a tramp steamer, heading off to God only knows where, strong and willing to meet adventure head on. I just knew in my ideal world that when it was time to check out, it should be in a gale in the wicked Tasman Sea or fighting pirates off the coast of Java. Of course, all along I also knew these dreams for what they were—just dreams. For I've never been brave, and since early in life I've been a person beset with low-grade anxiety and extra caution. And although in real life, I was an average person, struggling with the day-to-day as best I could, with the passing of the years the dreams refused to die.

From the moment of my "assignment," my focus was the circumnavigation. So I immediately took sailing lessons. And miracle of miracles, despite having never been aboard a sailboat in my entire life, I loved it! My mantra was, "Don't screw this up." But I felt more daring than ever before—even slightly reckless—and I was an eager student and always tried, and sometimes I did it right.

I also read everything I could on choosing a boat for bluewater cruising, even wading my way through technical magazines and pretending I understood or was interested in their mathematical formulas for calculating this and that. The best books were those about other people who had already done a circumnavigation. They fed my desire and belief in what could be. Now I had a mental canvas on which to draw my own dreams.

Soon I was spending my weekends walking the docks in the Clear Lake marina area, south of Houston, Texas, and the nearest yachting center. I looked at every boat advertised that might fit my needs and talked to all the brokers I could, even though all but one said the same thing: "Why don't you get a nice bay boat and try it, then if you like it you can always buy another." More than once I heard, "You know, little lady (they actually say that in Texas), for every 10,000 who say they will sail around the world, only one does," which just made me mad and strengthened my determination to go. All along I knew I had a secret weapon—my destiny. I did what I could to try to glean some solid knowledge from them as I searched. Most important of all, I steadfastly kept to my mission.

Ultimately I was fortunate enough to find just the right boat, a 32-foot Allied Seawind ketch, something I could handle by myself, since at the time I figured I would be alone. This was an older boat, but solid, with a heavy full keel. And the things that needed to be done were things that I could handle. I found the boat through a friend of a friend, and it seemed to fit my limited budget. It was not officially for sale, but someone had heard that the owner might want to sell it.

The first time I looked at it, the owner had just finished installing a new water tank and a new cabin sole. When I asked him for a price, it seemed like it was pretty high for such an old boat that still needed lots of upgrades. But he sounded very firm, so I told him I would have to think about it. At the time, the interior was all torn up, and though I could sort of see through the sawdust, I was too new at this to *really* see through the sawdust. I looked around a bit more at some other prospects, but all the while this boat was on my mind. This was a boat that could sail around the world. I finally admitted it. *I wanted that boat.* When I called back 10 days later, the owner had raised the price another $3,000. "I have put more work into it, so it's worth more now." Rats! He had a real take-it-or-leave-it tone of voice. I don't know what kind of negotiations I could have pursued, but I was already hooked and helpless. I said okay, and the deed was done.

Oh, heaven! Anyone who has bought a sailboat knows the adoration, excitement and dreams that are attached to that piece of floating fiberglass, and I was no different. My dream had only been growing for two years, but it had sprung full-blown, so it was as if it had been there all my life. I named her ALEXANDRA, a name that to me is full of meaning. ALEXANDRA!

It's a name that seems to hold all the adventure, romance and glory of my destiny in one word.

Of course, naming a boat was one thing. Preparing that same boat to sail around the world was another matter entirely. At the time I bought ALEXANDRA, I traveled frequently with my job, and it slowed down any work on the boat. Also, though the pre-purchase survey told me what needed to be done, I had no idea how to do it. Every project, no matter how small, required that I first read a book that explained what to do, then ask neighbors and friends lots of questions, then decide whether I could do it myself or have it hired out. Like most sailors, money was most definitely an object, so it was slow going. The first time I put in an electrical outlet on my own, I felt quite proud. (I'm *pretty* sure I did it right.) But I didn't try anything that might impact the structural integrity of the boat. Replacing the dry-rotted mizzenmast support, for example, went to someone who knew what he was doing.

Next I went really crazy and moved on board. Ah, the feeling of coziness and warmth. The smallness made it feel like a nest. I still love that feeling: a cocoon, bundling, the womb. Probably very Freudian, but there you are.

As time went on, another strange thing happened. I didn't want to be alone anymore. Now *that* was a new feeling! Here I'd been single for almost 20 years, content in that status. Now, at the age of 49, when the pool of available men was growing ever smaller, I'd finally decided that it was time for a partner again. Oh great! What's that so-called statistic? A woman is more likely to be struck by lightning than to marry after 40?

Some time earlier, when I had been lamenting the fact that I was meeting less and less single men, a friend had suggested a dating service or a singles ad—an idea I had soundly rejected. But then one day I had a brainstorm—why not take it one step further? Why not put an ad in *Cruising World* magazine? That way I would meet only people interested in sailing, and I could specify exactly what I wanted. If there was no one out there like that, then I would know it right away. If there *was* someone, maybe fortune would smile on me. Since the partner business wasn't in my message from God, I didn't have the same confidence in this tactic. But surely no sailor could be a psychopath. Naive me, I have since learned differently, but that's another story.

My brainstorm occurred during lunchtime at work, so I called my oldest daughter, Alecia, who is not only my daughter, but also one of my best friends.

"Go for it, Mom," she said. So I called *Cruising World* magazine, and they told me to fax my ad in right away since that very day was the deadline for an upcoming issue. Okay, I thought, here goes: *Attractive 49 y/o lady sailor is seeking a SWM of same generation as friend/possible permanent partner, for cruising future and beyond. The oceans are waiting. I don't want to go alone!* I didn't use the "m" word. I still wasn't sure that marriage was what I wanted. I signed it, "Alexandra," and before I knew it everything was settled. I gulped, hoped I wasn't too nuts, and forgot about it.

2

&

All the Willing Men

Two months later I found out how many single men of my generation were also looking for a sailing partner. Within three weeks of the issue hitting the newsstands, I received 125 letters. They came from all over the United States and Canada. All nice letters, no weird ones. Well, except maybe for one. He opened with, "Hey Babe, where you been all my life?" So I tossed that one in the trash. Oh, and there was another man who sent a nice letter, but then told me over the phone that he liked his women "perfect." Curious, I asked, "What does perfect mean? " I had a feeling plump was out. He said, "Perfect figure, perfect face. In fact, even perfect feet." Now, I think my feet are pretty cute, but I'm probably the only one, so we never met.

Actually, it was all quite overwhelming. I hadn't expected this and didn't even want that kind of response. I tried answering the letters as they came in, but soon gave up. There were too many, with too much information about people who were strangers to me. My daughters were great. They would read them and give me their opinion. I decided to respond to the most promising letters with the statement that I wanted to sail around the world and I wanted to get married. "If you are not interested in both of these," I wrote, "no need to write back." Most of the men I wrote to with that message did respond back. They all seemed to think that marriage would be nice, but sailing around the world was pretty daunting. Personally, I thought sailing around the world would be a piece of cake compared to being married.

Then came the letter from Dave, a widower who had been married for 42 years to the same woman, loving her all that time. Obviously he knew something about maintaining a happy marriage, having already done it once, and he was interested in a circumnavigation and the possibility of another marriage. He sounded like a nice person. My daughters thought his picture was cute. So I wrote back.

In the end it took us several more months to meet, but we exchanged letters and phone calls that entire time. I did meet a few others. But while they were all nice, none seemed the right person for me. And they seemed to feel the same way. One fellow sounded fun and interesting on the phone, but when he came to visit, he was distant and cool. Later when I called him, he reported, "Well, I didn't hear any bells, if you know what I mean," which was fine with me, although I really think he could have found a less ego-crushing excuse. Granted, I didn't hear bells either, but that was beside the point.

One man I talked to on the telephone said to me, "Wow, you really know what you want. You are very specific!" I replied honestly, "Yes, I know exactly what I want, and I won't settle for less!" Who *was* this person speaking with such confidence and determination?

Another fellow sent a beautiful set of watercolors of his boat along with a lovely letter about warm sunsets and sleepy lagoons—very imaginative and romantic. But when we talked, I quickly realized the letter was a sales pitch. He was looking for a partner to buy into his boat so it wouldn't be so expensive for him.

Alas, it seemed I was no longer a young, attractive divorcee, flitting easily from man to man. Instead, I was now a middle-aged, slightly overweight grandmother who didn't flit so well. In my head I was still that young, pretty woman, but apparently the men saw differently. Hmmm, this wasn't going to be easy.

It was with these thoughts in the back of my head that at the end of January 1993, Dave and I arranged to meet. He was living on his boat TIGGER, a Tartan 37, in Florida. He drove to Houston where he got a hotel room, intending to stay for the weekend. We met on a Friday night for dinner.

As he greeted me in the hotel lobby, I saw a nice looking man, not much taller than me, wearing a navy blazer, with a crewcut and lots of laugh lines. So far, so good. I shook his hand and smiled. I drove us to the restaurant, since I felt I was in charge of this interview. That's the way I had to view meeting these strangers; it was too stressful if I thought of it as a *date*. Over dinner we began by talking about our boats, our children, our careers (his as an instrumentation engineer, retired eight years before), and our hobbies (his composing music and conducting). I learned later that Dave was an accomplished pianist. Our boat is almost always filled with music, classical and opera, and if you stop by, you may find him wildly conducting a recording of a Beethoven symphony or Bach's *St. Matthew's Passion*. I already knew that he was 15 years older than I was, so we weren't exactly of the same generation. But I was willing to overlook that fact and so was he.

I was still feeling a bit cautious the next day when he appeared, electric drill in hand, to announce that if I would haul him up the mast, he would install my windvane, then go up the mizzen and check the triatic stay. Whoa, this guy instinctively knew how to reach my heart! That night after dinner, we sat in the car and talked about ourselves, our real selves. "The thing I miss most now that my children are grown," I told him, "is skin touch. I have so little of that now. I used to be able to hold them, and they would snuggle with me and we would have that gentle maternal contact. It feels cold now, my skin feels so cold." Dave told me about missing his wife, about her illness, the overpowering grief after she was gone. He was so easy to talk with, to share thoughts and feelings with. We were becoming friends.

He came for the weekend, but on Monday he decided to stay another day, ostensibly to see the nearby Johnson Space Center. That night I got back to ALEXANDRA after work, and there were flowers on the fold-down table and dinner was cooking. This guy was good! On Tuesday, he decided there was a park that he would like to see before he left. That night there was another dinner and more flowers waiting. After dinner, as we were talking, he casually mentioned he was falling in love with me. *Oh boy*, what do I do now? Actually, I was in free-fall myself! We began talking of marriage as if it were a foregone conclusion. Later, alone on the boat after Dave had gone back to his hotel, I sort of "checked in" with my heart to see how it was doing. It was doing cartwheels. I took that as a good sign.

That first Sunday he was there, I took him to Houston to meet my three children and their respective partners. They dutifully gathered round, gave him the once over, and tentatively approved of Mom's date. I doubt if they thought at that time that I would be calling with our engagement announcement several days later. But whatever misgivings they had, they saw my happiness and his gentle attentions, and nodded an approval.

Dave finally left to go back to Florida and tend to TIGGER. I was to come several days later, taking vacation time from work, so that we could sail to the Dry Tortugas for a holiday. The Dry Tortugas consist of several small islands at the very western tip of the Florida Keys, 75 miles from Key West. We could sail the distance in one day, have several days there and then sail back, after which I could go back to Houston and work until we decided what next.

When we got to Key West we said, "What the heck, let's make the Dry Tortugas our honeymoon," which is how I found out just how easy the State of Florida makes it to get married—just a license and someone to marry you! No blood test, no waiting period, no nothing. When we tied up at the Truman Marina in Key West, we found it was still under construction, not much in the way of facilities. But to me, it seemed both romantic and very representative of my future life. Dave mentioned to the dockmaster that we wanted to get married and asked if he knew where we could find a justice of the peace.

"No problem," the dockmaster said. "We have a notary public right here, and she is authorized to perform marriage ceremonies."

"Fine," Dave said. We had both agreed we wanted a civil ceremony only.

Off we went to the license bureau, where after less than 30 minutes we emerged with a marriage license. As it turned out, our timing was perfect. Right after we got ours, a cruise ship came in and there was a long line of couples waiting for licenses so they could marry in Key West too.

On our way back to the marina we bought a bouquet of yellow roses to match my wedding attire. I wore Key West chic that day: yellow shorts and a yellow-and-green tropical-print shirt. Dave, being more conservative, wore his best shirt and shorts. We walked into the marina office and Dave told the young girl behind the desk that we were there to get married.

"What?" she asked.

"The dockmaster told us the notary public here could marry us," Dave said, as the girl grew noticeably paler.

"Oh no, I can't marry you!" she said. "I'm the notary public, but I can't marry you."

"Why?" I asked.

"Because I am not experienced enough," she said. "I've only had my license a short time. I've never married anyone. It wouldn't be right. I haven't even memorized the words. No, I just can't do it," she concluded firmly.

Dave, however, was not going to be deterred. "Well, just sign the paper then, we really don't need a ceremony, we are happy just to make it legal."

But this wouldn't do either. Carolyn fretted and stewed, and then finally rummaged through her desk until she found the "marriage card" that was part of her notary packet, which she triumphantly held up before us. "No, you can't do it that way, the words must be said. I've got this card, I can do it," she declared, adding that she would be ready in 30 minutes. Now she was getting in the spirit of things! The dockmaster swung into action and dug out a bottle of champagne, a leftover from the New Year's party. Since he had a great camera, he would be the official photographer.

Down to TIGGER we went. It was a bright and sunny day, with white puffy clouds being pushed by brisk winds across a deep blue sky. The waters around the marina were turquoise, and outside the breakwater the bay was alive with whitecaps.

Carolyn and Dave stood in the cockpit. The dockmaster was on the dock with his camera to get just the right shots.

Carolyn reading the "marriage card", Key West

And I walked down the aisle by climbing up the companion-way ladder, carrying my yellow roses. Carolyn was in a tizzy of excitement and nervousness, but as she started reading the marriage vows, it all came together and made sense and felt right. Love is a strange and wonderful thing, and it infected all of us that afternoon, with the wind wrapping our happiness around us.

Back in Texas, although only three weeks had passed since Dave and I had first met, my children were shocked but thrilled and happy for us. My friends couldn't believe I was the same cynical person who vowed to stay single and once looked sadly at any woman who was getting married. "Poor thing, she's in for trouble!" I'd lament. It is a measure of my friends' and family's love for me that they didn't make me eat my words.

Dave's three children, on the other hand, were not so easy. They lived in different parts of the country, and they had never met me. Also, they were still grieving the loss of their mother two and a half years before and were very protective of their father. Dave and I felt a bit like we had sneaked away from our parents to marry. We had to remind ourselves several times that *we* were the parents.

Looking back on it, I wouldn't recommend our speedy courtship to anyone else, but fast though it may have been, it was perfect for us, and Dave does indeed know how to maintain a happy marriage. He is my best friend, and falling in love and marrying him was the easiest thing I've ever done. I never for a moment doubted that it was the right thing—a real first for me. And all these years later, I still congratulate myself on my good choice and good fortune.

As I tell people our story, it sounds weird to me too, and I always tell it awkwardly. But there you are, life is so full of things that don't make sense. Some of them just happen to be miracles.

Amazingly, after the first passion had settled down (and settle down it did, in a most delightful way), it still turned out to be a good match. Our personalities are well suited to each other. I am strong-minded and independent, but nice—really. He is quiet and appears mild-mannered to the casual observer, but beneath it all, he is one stubborn guy. He's also smart and funny. We laugh a lot and are never bored with each other. He's extremely kind to me. I like that.

A month later we sailed TIGGER to Houston and prepared to sell my house and my beloved ALEXANDRA, since Dave's boat was not only bigger and better outfitted for cruising, but it had been Dave's home for the past 10 years. It wasn't easy selling ALEXANDRA—she was the symbol of my dream—but I had Dave now, and though the dream was the same, I wasn't alone anymore. I had already told my very surprised employer that I was married, that I was going to sail around the world, and goodbye. Then Dave and I settled in for the six-month task of preparing TIGGER for the long haul.

3

Let the Voyage, and the Marriage, Begin

We left Galveston, Texas, in December of 1993, trying to catch the tail end of one of the region's northers to push us south and east before the normal east and southeast winds of December took over. Our first stop would be Isla Mujeres, at the tip of the Yucatán Peninsula, 640 miles southeast of Galveston. From Isla Mujeres, it would be mostly coastal sailing along Central America to Panama. After that would be the long trek westward across the Pacific Ocean.

It took two days to clear all the oil rigs and dodge the shrimp boats roaming the Gulf waters off Galveston. At the end of two days, the weather was bright and sunny, and we exchanged our winter jackets and sweaters for the shorts and T-shirts that would be our standard dress—when we bothered to wear anything—for the rest of the trip.

In fact, the calm weather continued, and never did turn into the rough trip we had expected. The forecast on the SSB radio had predicted that a low to the south of us would bring rough seas and 30-knot winds. But it never materialized and the trip was a piece of cake. The benign weather did our hearts good. For we were not yet the tough, offshore sailors that we would hopefully be someday.

Four days out and we were boarded by pirates! Well, not pirates exactly, although they certainly looked the part. At the time we were about 70 miles northwest of the Isla Contoy lighthouse, marking the northern entrance to the Yucatán Channel. It was a lovely sunny day—no wind, blue skies and a mirror for the sea. Not what we expected, but we weren't complaining. This being December, it could have been very bad in the Gulf.

I was on watch, just lazing about, letting TIGGER drift after having motored until the noise was driving us mad, when I saw a black speck on the horizon. As I watched, the speck got bigger and bigger, until I could tell it was a dory of some kind and coming fast. I didn't like the looks of this. I called Dave and told him he should come up. I also ran below and got our weapons of choice, a small flare gun about the size of a cigar and a small knife with the serrated edge. Don't scoff at the tiny flare gun. We once shot one of the pencil-like flares as a test and it streaked across the lagoon with so much power it would have gone right through anyone in its path. Thus armed, we waited as up they came, right up to the boat, in an old and beat-up dory with a big engine—not new, but big. The crew had nothing on except dingy, brief underwear, and they were as brown and scruffy as the boat. We all eyed each other while I kept low in the companionway, hiding my weapon and peering out. Then one of the men reached down to the bottom of the dory and pulled out a fish! They were fishermen and wanted to sell or trade part of their catch. Since neither Dave nor I speak Spanish and they didn't speak English, there was a moment of tension. But then I popped up from my hiding spot, and we took advantage of our first chance to trade with some locals. After much pantomime and talk, we settled for a red fish weighing about three pounds, which Dave said he thought was a snapper. We had no pesos, so we offered them two dollars and three Cokes. Since there were three of them, that seemed to be a fair trade and off they went, disappearing over the horizon.

I was now feeling quite chipper, what with my first successful trade. Even though I really butchered that poor fish and only managed to salvage about six ounces of edible flesh, it was fish and rice for dinner. About halfway through our meal, I had one of my little anxiety attacks over the fact that I really didn't know if this was a snapper or not, and there was the chance I might get sick. Was this such a good idea? Were my lips a little numb, a sure sign of ciguatera poisoning? Dave looked the fish up in our fish book. But even though it sure looked like a snapper, I finished the rice and Dave finished the fish. Throughout our trip I sometimes used Dave as a taste-tester for food that was questionable to my fertile imagination. If he survived, then I would have it for leftovers the next day. The system worked well.

We spotted the Isla Contoy lighthouse at dusk the next day, right where it should be, which was a big relief for me. This was only my second time offshore and the first relying exclusively on GPS for navigating. With no landmarks, no coast, nothing but sea and sky, seeing this light confirmed that I was still in the same world I had left almost six days before. What a comfort. We chose to stand off Isla Mujeres until dawn when we felt more comfortable entering the narrow reef opening leading to the marina and adjacent anchorage.

There were several marinas, but Dave chose the one nearest to the town, which was small and quiet with a little thatched gazebo right on the dock. We tied up three days before Christmas in front of five big shrimp boats that were also having a Christmas respite. As exotic as these boats appeared, the flies they attracted were not, and we swatted and sprayed and tied plastic bags of water in the companionway to keep them at bay the entire time we were there. What were the water bags supposed to do, you ask? I'm not sure, but the explanation was that if a fly saw itself in the reflection it wouldn't come in. It did help, and I only broke two bags of water in the galley during our comings and goings.

Isla Mujeres, or "Island of Women," is a touristy little village across the bay from Cancún, full of cantinas, dive shops and waterfront restaurants. The village is Mexican shabby, which means it's neat and clean, but the buildings, both adobe and wood, don't get painted very often. It had a main square near the church, where young people played basketball, and adults sat and visited. What a great people-watching spot!

We were intending to make Panama by April so we were going to have to hurry down the coast. But soon after we arrived, Dave began talking with a neighbor who had refrigerator problems. Dave commented that he'd had his refrigerator on TIGGER for 18 years and it worked like a charm. Of course, after that it quit working within three hours, so we had to wait 15 days for parts.

We still had a lot to learn about foreign ports. We were at a restaurant along the waterfront for New Year's Day dinner. Since we are generally early to bed, we planned on an early dinner, having walked the mile or so to town. Dave ordered a margarita and said it tasted kind of funny. I tried it, but it tasted fine to me. (Being a nondrinker, what did I know?) He started getting silly about the time dinner was over. And 10 minutes later, as we were walking the dark path back to the boat, he was skipping. Then came the singing, "I am drunk, yippee, I am drunk." Since we'd been married less than a year, I began wondering if there wasn't more to Dave than I had thought. But he was a happy drunk, and laughed and skipped and sang his way back to the marina.

Back at the marina, we approached a group of affluent looking Mexicans having a party on the dock, next to their big motoryacht. I told Dave, "Whatever you do, don't make a fool of yourself in front of these people." After which he promptly fell down with his head hanging over the edge of the dock, hand dangling in the water. The fellow who owned the million-dollar yacht jumped up and came to his rescue, pulling him up and holding him to keep him from falling again. Since the whole party was staring at Dave, I explained, "He's drunk." But apparently, they didn't speak English because they just looked at me. So I said, "Tequila." And they all nodded solemnly and said "Ahhh, tequila." It seemed to explain everything. With some help, I got Dave on the boat and then down below, still singing, at least until about three seconds after his head hit the pillow. Then he was out cold. I spent some time that night thinking about the surprises that can occur in a marriage.

The next day was another story. He was very hung over and sick. When I told our friends about the episode, thinking it all very funny by now, they said they were pretty sure he had been slipped a Mickey in preparation for a mugging on the way home. Something must have stopped the muggers, but it wasn't us. If ever there were a couple of chickens ripe for plucking, it was the two of us.

The Mexicans are such polite people. And they always want to accommodate, even when they can't. We went shopping one day in Cancún, having taken the ferry across the bay. We were looking for zinc for the propeller shaft. Again, our Spanish is pretty limited and our vocabularies did not include the word zinc (which apparently is zinc), and no one seemed to speak English where we were. We would ask if they had zinc, and they would nod as if they understood, then shake their heads and point to the store down the street. We would go to the store they had pointed to, and repeat. The proprietors of that establishment would nod first, then shake their heads and direct us farther down the street and around the corner. Then off we'd go again. We repeated this enough times that we finally found ourselves back where we had started! No one ever shrugged and said, "I don't know." They just wanted so much to be able to help.

There are two ferries that cross the bay to Cancún, one fast and one slow. The slow one takes twice as long, but you get to keep your kidneys and eardrums. The fast one is wet, rough and you feel like you're riding in the tail section of a 727 through a bad storm. We had to try both, but only once. The slow one gets my vote.

Finally, after the 15 days of waiting for refrigerator parts turned to 20, we were off again and moving on down the coast.

As we passed the Mayan ruin of Tulum, perched on the cliff above the sea, I remarked to Dave, "I bet a lot of maidens were thrown off that cliff." He answered, "No, I don't think they threw anyone over the cliff, I think the Mayans ripped the still-beating hearts out of their sacrificial maidens." Hmm, either way, the maidens had a tough time of it.

Our first anchorage was Hut Point where we tucked in behind a reef and stayed for four days while the winds blew 40 knots out of the northeast. There is nothing so snug as being dug in behind a reef in calm water, while outside the reef the seas and sky are wild. I played solitaire for hours, read, watched the seas and daydreamed about my good fortune.

A few days later, anchored farther south in Bahia de Ascension, our neighbors on MARIAH whom we had met in Isla Mujeres, had a party, so off we went in our Boston Whaler-style dinghy. It was heavier than most dinghies its size, but very stable. The swells were pretty high that afternoon. As I stood on the bow of the dinghy, preparing to step on MARIAH's boarding ladder, the dinghy dropped into a trough leaving me dangling in the air, one arm wrapped around the boarding ladder, but unable to get a good foothold on the rocking yacht. Eventually, the dinghy rose up on the next wave and hit my foot, practically catapulting me into the cockpit. Safe at last. After lots of good food and sailing stories, we headed home.

Since the wind was from the south it was pushing us downwind and toward TIGGER at a rapid rate. The outboard was on the fritz again, so I was rowing. Dave said, "Whatever you do, don't let us get past TIGGER, we'll never be able to row back upwind to her." After which, we were immediately swept past TIGGER, and Dave had to unceremoniously dump me forward, while he took over the rowing, now upwind and into the swells. With my plump body forward, we were taking waves over the bow like a scoop in a sugar bowl! When we finally got to our boat, the dinghy was just about swamped. But the water was warm and the shore was nearby, so what was the worry?

I still thought we could make it to Panama by April, but

we were moving slowly and Dave had a lot of places he wanted to see, so we took it easy and spent over a month getting through Belize. The weather was great: sunny days, with an almost constant southeast breeze. Sailing inside the reef in Belize is so easy, with a nice steady wind and no big seas. The water was shallow, 15 to 30 feet in most places. We anchored in the quiet bay at Cay Caulker for a while, then Cay Chapel, and then a small marina at Moho Cay so we could provision in Belize City.

We took a land trip to Tikal, the ancient Mayan ruins in northern Guatemala, flying in a small plane over the jungle. At Tikal, we climbed to the top of one pyramid, and found ourselves gazing over the top of the jungle canopy. In the distance were other ruins of this incredible city, also rising out of the jungle canopy. In the background was the music of the jungle—mysterious birds calling, and the *waaaa hoo hoo hoo, waaaa hoo hoo hoo* of the howler monkeys.

We went into Belize City for provisions on the day Queen Elizabeth was visiting. The whole country was atwitter, and

Resting after climbing the pyramid, Tikal, Guatemala

the children got the day off from school. We took a taxi to town, and the driver told us all about Her Majesty's schedule that day. People were already lining the roads, waiting for her motorcade. On the way back, our driver took us on the route the queen would be taking in an hour. At one spot, there were about 300 schoolchildren lined up, all waving small British flags. For some reason, as we started by, they began waving their flags and cheering. So Dave doffed his hat to each side of the road, and I gave a royal wave. As we slowly moved along, the children cheered and waved, and we smiled and waved and felt quite regal. So that's how the queen does it!

After that we continued south, sailing with a headsail only, the wind filling our 150-percent genoa. Sunshine, blue skies— it was a glorious time of gentle sailing and safe anchorages.

Still I was very ready to get offshore again. Even though we'd come across the Gulf of Mexico, I didn't yet feel like I'd had enough deepwater experience to be considered a "real" sailor. I was also anxious to get far enough away from the United States so that I'd know we were going to circle the globe. It seemed such a fantastic mission, that unless we were working toward that goal each day, I was afraid it would just disappear, and I would find myself in Houston, waking up from a dream.

Dave on the other hand wasn't half so anxious, and there were many spirited discussions about how fast we should go and what we were missing by hurrying. I tried, I really did, but there it was, the fear that it wasn't real. I just had to get far enough that turning around wasn't an option. Dave said that I would always be like this—wanting to hurry, never satisfied with now. And I even thought I heard him mutter the word "pushy" once or twice, although I probably got that wrong. Luckily, he was also understanding and we both tried to compromise in our attitudes.

4

✍

The Rio Dulce, Guatemala

The Rio Dulce is a lovely river that runs some 40 miles in-land from the southeast coast of Guatemala to Lago de Iz-abal, a huge lake in the jungle. Near the entrance to Lago de Izabal are several small marinas, along with the well-preserved remains of a fort. Here the Spanish used to come to fill their ships with plundered goods from the fabulous treasures of Central America. The fort stood guard, but I thought it strange to have it so far upriver. Why not have it at the entrance to the river and never let the enemy get any farther?

There's a sandy bar across the river entrance at Livingston that sailboats could cross only at high tide. We had heard via the cruisers' radio net that you could get a fisherman to haul you across if you did get stuck, but TIGGER's draft is less than five feet so we decided to do the high tide option and be safe. We made it across easily, with at least six inches under the bottom of the keel. Then we anchored inside the bar and called Customs on the VHF radio to let them know we were there. Soon the officials arrived and after some paperwork and small talk—no easy thing as they didn't speak English and we still didn't speak Spanish—they took our passports and told us to pick them up at the customs office in two hours.

Livingston is a small town at the edge of the river and backed by the jungle. As we landed our dinghy at the dock, several teen-age boys came over to watch it for us while we were gone. Pushing and shoving each other out of the way so they could each be first, they didn't look too trustworthy and Dave didn't want to give them money. But we decided a dollar was a small price to pay if it meant we would still see our dinghy there when we got back.

We got our passports back with little fuss. However, there were soldiers everywhere, the customs office also being a garrison for their army. The men were polite, but not friendly, and they were all so young! It was so sad to see these young men, boys really. This was another of the very real sorrows of the civil war going on down there at the time. At least the dinghy was still there when we got back to the dock.

The next morning we started the 30-mile run up the river. What an incredible motoring trip—each bend revealing another beautiful sight. In places, the river wound through a canyon with high cliffs on each side and the jungle tumbling down from above. Sometimes we'd pass near a shore, the jungle reaching right to the water's edge. Here and there was a curl of smoke from houses hidden from view by the thick green foliage. The scene was so peaceful, with only the hum of our engine to break the silence. If only there had been a bit of wind so we could put up sails and silence the engine, then we could have heard the birds, too.

Despite the fact that the Rio Dulce with its beauty and peace had sounded like a perfect cruising ground, for me it was a combination of beauty and misery. There are several marinas upriver, where the river joins Lago de Izabal, in the area near the small village of Fronteras, and we'd chosen Mario's Marina because it was recommended to us by several cruisers. It was in a lovely setting, but crowded with boats four deep and a spider web of lines running from boat to shore, boat to boat, shore to boat. We were so close to our neighbor that only the fenders kept us apart. It was also March—hot and humid.

As we got farther from the sea, my back muscles started tightening, a sure sign of stress. Then I started getting a strange feeling of foreboding. It was heavy and dark. This didn't feel right. Dave and my daughter Erika, who had joined us in Belize for this part of the trip, thought I was weird. I *felt* weird. For the first four days at the marina I was flat on my back in the V-berth with back strain. While I was feeling sorry for myself, the other two promptly got the Rio Dulce virus, 24 to 48 hours of misery, accompanied by fever, vomiting and diarrhea. Then as soon as my back got better, it was my turn. Talking to others in the marina, they said everyone who came to this place got it at least once. Why would anyone deliberately choose a place that guaranteed several days of vomiting and diarrhea every so often? I was ready to leave. I cried. I argued. I pleaded. Finally Dave said, "Okay, let's go." But then I heard there was a fellow who would make a new dodger for us, which we sorely needed, so we stayed and had a new one made.

Three weeks later we sailed back downriver while Erika stayed behind to crew on another yacht. Setting our sails in open water was like being let out of prison. I could breathe again, safe and free. Maybe it was the cholera in the river, or the civil war still going on, or the poverty in this perfect setting. Perhaps it was the rich Guatemalans in their loud power-boats, or the fact that no one seemed to smile in Fronteras, the nearby village. It was not a place for me.

Our next stop was the Bay Islands, off the north coast of Honduras. Surely, I thought, with just a short stop in Roatán we could still make it to Panama in time for this year's crossing to the Marquesas. I was counting on it. It was a hard beat into a 20-knot northeast wind until just before the island of Roatán, but TIGGER did it in 36 hours, and as we sailed along the south shore of the island, the water was so clear I saw the bottom at 80 feet. No wonder this is a diver's paradise.

French Harbor was our destination with its snug little harbor, landlocked except for a narrow entrance channel. It has both a marina and an anchorage. But we must have had the cruising guide upside down, because we took a marker stake to port instead of starboard and found ourselves aground. And those were rocks beneath us! The wind was out of the east now, and the water was a bit choppy. We ran up and down the deck muttering, "Damn, damn," as the keel and rudder hit the bottom with each swell. Several cruisers came by in a dinghy and suggested that we put up some sail, saying it would make us heel, and that we would have more water under us to maneuver. Wrong move. With the sail up, we just sailed farther up onto the rocks. Down came the sail. We tried backing up under power, but TIGGER didn't budge. A fishing boat came by and asked if we wanted him to pull us off. "Yes," we cried, thinking this local would have the secret to getting us out of there. We used one of our good, stout lines, and he tied one end to our stern and the other to his stern, with the intention of pulling us backwards. He pulled and pulled and broke the towing line and still we were hard aground among the rocks. People were now all around us in dinghies and dugouts, all giving suggestions, all talking at once. Then two young boys paddled up in their kid-size dugout canoe and asked if we wanted them to dive on the bottom. Now why didn't we think of that? We were in four feet of water, we could have stood on the bottom and put our faces in the water! They went under and reported that the only thing stopping us was a big rock behind the rudder. With that new information, the fishing boat pulled us slightly forward, which brought the bow to starboard, and then maneuvered TIGGER around the obstacle until we were in the deeper water. Only sailors who have run their boat on the rocks can know the immense feeling of relief that comes when you're back in water deeper than the keel. We were quite lavish in our thanks and monetary rewards to both those two boys and the fisherman. Then we sheepishly motored into French Harbor and took a place at the dock.

Since we had bounced a few times during the grounding, Dave checked the bilge as soon as we docked. We weren't taking on any water, but on the outside of the hull, we could see a small fracture above the waterline at the extreme stern. On the Tartan 37 the rudder is directly below this point and for some reason the fiberglass is quite thin. Once before when we had run aground, the aft tip of the rudder had bounced up and hit that very same spot and put a fracture in the fiberglass in the same way. It's actually above the waterline, but as the stern settles lower in the water when underway, it leaks. So Dave filled the thin spot from the inside with epoxy, putting it on good and thick, so that it would never leak again. We even took a trial spin. No leak.

Since French Harbor was supposed to be just a stop on the way to Panama, we took off after four days, intending a daysail to Guanaja, the easternmost island in the group, making that our last land before rounding the tip of Honduras and heading south to Panama. Four miles out of French Harbor, however, we looked in the bilge. We were taking on water again! So back we went, this time taking the dreaded stake to starboard.

We realized the damage was more serious than we'd originally thought and that TIGGER would have to be hauled out in order for a repair to be done properly. Unfortunately, the only haulout facilities on the island were in the midst of their busy time since the shrimp boats were all being readied for the upcoming season. So we considered ourselves fortunate when Seth Arch, the owner of one of the facilities, said he would take us over the weekend and do the job if we paid his guys to work overtime.

Shortly thereafter we sailed onto his submerged marine railway cradle in 35 knots of wind, with his men all tugging on lines to pull us in while one dove on the cradle to position us. These fellows certainly knew their job. Then slowly we were pulled out of the water and onto land, with us on the boat. Pretty nerve wracking, but what a great view. Over the weekend they fiberglassed several spots of damage (the aft end of the keel had also taken a beating), painted the bottom and cut another intake hole in the hull so we could install a watermaker. By Monday morning we were back in the water. They had done a practical job, not pretty, but we should never have a leak in that spot again, and the bottom paint ought to last a year. They were used to working on steel-hulled fishing boats where the idea of a smooth sanding before bottom paint must not be the norm. But it was only $235 for all the work and the haulout, so I figure we got more than our money's worth.

Meanwhile Dave's middle daughter had just had her first child, and he was feeling pretty blue over the fact that he wasn't there for the arrival. So we took three weeks off and went back to the United States to visit. We'd only been gone four months, but I was also homesick so this was just what I needed, even though it was going to delay our arrival in Panama even more.

I was homesick and that was that. I know for some, it's never a problem. In fact it came as a big surprise to me since my dream was so strong, my mission so firm in my mind and heart. But there it was. Every now and then I would get into a low-grade depression that would last for days at a time, all as a result of missing family so much.

I remember a friend who went cruising just before we did. She had never been away from her family—mother, children and grandchildren, and she was having a very hard time saying goodbye. I am ashamed to say that at the time I told her, "How can you be so unhappy? You are going on a dream cruise, get with it!" I mentally ate those words many times. I get it now. I wanted to do this, I had to do it, but that didn't mean it was always going to be easy.

5

❦

Definitely Panama Bound

It was the middle of May when we finally left Roatán, bound
for Panama. We were uncertain whether to stop at Isla
Providencia, Colombia, which was directly on our path, so we
started out and would decide when we got near it.

Our course required an easterly heading until we could
round the northeast tip of Honduras. Then we'd head south,
gingerly dodging all the shoal areas that litter those waters. We
had a fresh south-southeast wind the first few days, which
made for a great sail, and we bounded along at 6 knots under
sunny skies with no leaks and both TIGGER and crew feeling
pretty frisky. When we rounded the corner to head south, it
would be worrisome for Dave, what with all the shoals and the
heavy shipping traffic in those waters. But for the time being
it felt quite pleasant.

It was on this first leg, though, that I was on watch and saw
a half-submerged steel container pass by only about 15 feet off
our port side. It must have fallen off a ship somewhere nearby,
and it gave me a chill. Why didn't we hit it, I wondered? Why
hadn't it been 15 feet over and directly in front of us? What
quirk of fate had permitted us to pass by unscathed? Would we
be as lucky in the future?

Since then I've had thoughts about flotsam more than a few times, but we've been lucky and always missed the floating hard stuff. What I finally had to come to terms with was the fact that it would either be there or not, and there's nothing I could do about it. I could control some things, but not that. So I let it go, kept some "safety prayers" tucked away somewhere, and got on with things.

Shortly thereafter we turned the corner and headed south. Now the wind was more easterly, and we were making good time toward Isla Providencia. There it was, right in our path and too convenient to resist. Our original reason for not stopping was that we'd heard it cost $200 to check in. But that sounded too bad to be true. So we raised the Colombian courtesy flag and the quarantine flag and sailed into the harbor.

Good decision. The bay was big and well protected, the water was flat even in 25 knots of wind, and there was good holding ground, once we got the anchor set properly. We put the dinghy in the water and went into town to check in with Mr. Bush, the Customs and Immigration agent. We paid $25 for his services and $35 for the check-in. It was worth it as he was cordial, and the check-in and check-out were painless. Walking back to the dinghy dock, however, TIGGER seemed farther away and closer to the entrance reef than before. Good God, she was closer. She was dragging! Our little two-horsepower outboard was never pushed so hard as that day, as we hurried out to try and catch TIGGER before she headed out to sea without us! It seems the bottom was sand and grass, and although we had anchored in only 15 feet of water, we couldn't see the bottom and all that grass, and our Bruce anchor always needs a little help in grass. Once we had rescued her and brought TIGGER back to where we were before, out went the Danforth as the second anchor, and from then on, no worries. In fact, we sat through almost 36 hours of 45-knot winds without a problem. The bay was flat, but the wind was howling. We were snuggly tucked at anchor and glad we were not yet on our way to Panama!

After that Dave and I set about taking a good look at Isla Providencia, which is easy because it's so small, maybe 15 miles in circumference. One day, we shared a taxi with some fellows from another yacht and took a tour of the island. The taxi was a small pickup truck with wooden benches built along the sides of the bed. That way you had an unimpeded view. The island was neat and clean, with colorful hand-painted political signs along the way. Apparently there was a hot contest going on, and education was the pivotal issue. Good for them. On the east side of the island, the road was high on the side of a hill, and we had a panoramic view of the reef and the Caribbean Sea beyond.

There were several sailboats in the anchorage, and one couple came to visit. They were from Malta, and the man was French. He spoke heavily accented English and with his accent, his age and his gestures, I thought I was in a vintage Maurice Chevalier movie. Very nice couple.

We set sail for Panama nine days later on a fair east-southeast breeze, although after we left the lee of the island, the winds picked up and so did the seas. That's when the seasickness kicked in. I always get seasick at the beginning of a passage. I'm not incapacitated, just nauseated, grouchy and lethargic. I've tried every remedy known to man, but they mostly make me feel worse than the mal de mer. So I've decided to just live with it, and after three or four days, it goes away. Dave knows not to cross me or I am likely to snarl, but I never miss a watch, and when something needs to be done, I can always do it.

Dave, the little darling, never gets seasick, no matter how rough it is. He can be happily cooking in the galley with no ill effects, while I stay on deck, trying not to catch a whiff of any of the cooking smells. No food for me, just lots of liquids, and when I finally get my sea legs back I am the happiest person on earth (and Dave the happiest man!).

The seas stayed rough, with squally, rain-laden southeast winds on the second day out that continued until we were within sight of Panama. There was a small leak where the mast came through the deck. Since we were heeling to starboard, that meant a drip of cold seawater every 20 seconds or so whenever we would lie down on the best sea berth. It was too rough to do any kind of repairs, and we were so tired by then, what with standing three-hour watches and never getting enough sleep, that we just put a towel across our chests and tried our best to rest. We hadn't toughened up as much as we would later in the journey. The time would come when we could sleep through anything. But this trip was pretty miserable.

Finally, however, we arrived in Panama one early afternoon in improved weather, motoring around the big anchored ships waiting their turn to enter the canal. What a thrill it was to arrive at last. Maybe we really would keep to my dream and sail around the world. We had only to pass through the canal and keep heading west, no obstacles after this.

Crossing from one ocean to another was quite significant for me. I felt a stranger in the Atlantic, but the Pacific was my home. I was born on the West Coast and had maintained a love affair with the South Pacific all my life. Now I was about to "really start the circumnavigation." To me the Caribbean signifies a cruising ground, but the wide Pacific signifies passagemaking. I had been so afraid I would wake up from this dream, and that if somehow I could just get to the Pacific Ocean, it would be real, a dream from which I wouldn't awaken. Now here I was on the brink of breaking through.

6

I Can Almost Smell the Pacific

As we slowly motored past The Flats, an anchorage for cruising yachts waiting to transit, and toward the Panama Canal Yacht Club, we toasted TIGGER and ourselves with my "emergency" Frangelico, a bottle of liqueur I had purchased before we left the United States. I am generally a nondrinker having overdone it a little in my "gay divorcee" days, but had thought back in Texas that there might be a time when I would need an emergency dose of courage. The trouble with that strategy was that when I needed the courage, we were usually too busy to have a shot. Then when the crisis was over, I didn't need it. But it was open now, and we both had a few self-congratulatory sips. When we toasted TIGGER and ourselves, our feeling of smugness was tempered by the knowledge that at any time it could all turn to mud. But for the moment, my body and soul were grinning.

Before taking your own boat through the canal it is recommended that you line-handle on another transiting yacht and since each yacht transiting is required to have four line-handlers, a helmsman and an advisor, the system works quite well. The line-handlers can be volunteers or hired hands, but the advisor is an employee of the Canal Authority. By volunteering to line-handle, you get a better understanding of the process, as well as a feel for being a small boat in among the huge freighters. Both of these experiences are worth having before bringing your own boat through. We volunteered to go with Arthur and Caroline on AQUARIUS and made it to our 6 a.m. schedule at the first lock. Unfortunately, Canal Control notified us that we would have to wait, first one hour, then another, and then finally they told us to go back to The Flats and prepare for a noon transit. Instead of The Flats, Caroline steered AQUARIUS back to the marina dock to wait. Caroline was skilled at the helm, and she kissed the dock lightly so we could tie up. After that we all relaxed until our noon appointment.

With all the big ships passing through the canal, small boats are not always handled right on schedule. Big ships have priority. We were told that over and over. But when we came back at noon, we quickly went through the first set of locks. Such a late start meant we could not transit in one day, and we spent the night anchored off Gamboa, halfway through the canal. The advisor got a ride with a pilot boat and went home for the night. The line-handlers—Caroline, one hired handler named Roy, Dave and I—slept on board and were ready early the next morning when the new advisor was delivered to AQUARIUS. The rest of the transit was uneventful, and we soon saw the welcome waters of the Bay of Panama and the Pacific Ocean.

Earlier we had purchased the book, *The Path Between the Seas*, by David McCullough, which we'd read before we arrived. It's a fascinating book about the building of the canal. It's not only about the incredible engineering feat, a marvel even today almost 100 years later, but a tale of disease, heat and the death of thousands. The workers had to deal with dysentery, malaria and yellow fever, as well as terrible accidents during the blasting and digging. If that weren't enough, there was the scheming and manipulations and millions of dollars spent behind the scenes—in short, the politics—and it gave our transit extra color and excitement to know some of the history of the canal. It's not necessarily a pretty story, but still one of great courage and vision.

As for making the actual transit, the first step is locking up, that is, going from sea level to the higher level of Gatun Lake in the middle of the canal. Then comes locking down, to the ocean on the other side. It's hard to describe what it feels like to be behind one of the big ships when locking up. There's so much power in this relatively small space. We were like helpless little cockleshells compared to the big brutes around us.

Mules are small locomotives that attach lines to the ships fore and aft. They are very powerful and from their rails along the top of the lock walls, they slowly move the ships in and out of the locks, so they don't have to maneuver themselves. Still the ships must put on a little bit of power to help the mules get them started and even that little bit causes the water to be churned up. Currents and eddies swirl around small yachts, with only the lines to the lock walls, or another rafted boat, to keep them from being tossed around and into the concrete.

When locking down, small boats are in front of the freighters, and the freighters pull up so close that their bows loom over you. You really hope the mules and the engines can stop them. I felt that only good luck and an unseen hand were between our boat and a major mishap. But at the same time, it was daring and exciting.

Colón is the city on the Caribbean side of the canal, and Panama City is on the Pacific side. Panama City is a relatively modern, civilized place but Colón is a hellhole. It seemed a city of poverty and despair. Muggings were a daily occurrence, and we heard of one man, a German, who had his finger cut off for his ring. Whether this was true we couldn't be sure. But when we went to provision, we called a taxi to pick us up in front of the yacht club, which took us directly to the door of the market where an armed guard outside the market opened the door for us as we rushed inside. In one supermarket, right in the middle of downtown, there were armed guards at the end of each aisle. Even more disturbing was the fact that these guards were 15-year-old kids! I have heard some cruisers say they liked Colón, but not very many. For me the city radiated darkness and despair.

We were ready to go 10 days later after waiting for parts for an engine repair. But when we needed line-handlers, no volunteers were available so we hired Roy, the handler we'd met earlier when we'd helped on AQUARIUS, and he brought along some others, including his younger brother whom we were told not to pay since he was here for the experience.

Luckily, we got an early and on-time start, so after the first lock, we pushed TIGGER at over 5 knots under power through Gatun Lake to the next lock. Our advisor took us on the short cut, not sanctioned, but faster, and we had no problems. During locking, we rafted up with a French yacht, and then our two yachts were centered in the middle of the lock as if they were one vessel. The portside lines went to the wall from the French boat and the starboard lines went to the opposite wall

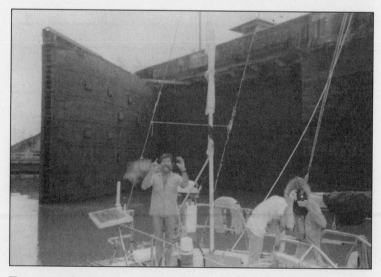

Transiting the Panama Canal, rafted up with a French yacht

from our boat. The idea was to hold the lines evenly tight from the bow and stern of each yacht. When the water level went up, the lines would be taken in. When it went down, the lines would be let out. Our French friend was all business at 6 a.m., and at our first lock all went well. But he was drinking something out of a big cup, which I mistakenly thought was coffee and as the day proceeded, things on the French boat got a little more lax. When he neglected to tend his lines and we shouted for him to let them out or take them in, we got the famous French shrug and a big smile and laugh. Then his girl-friend, Angelique, would run to take care of things. Whatever he was drinking made him happier and more oblivious (and Angelique busier) as the trip went on. Throughout this process he wore nothing more than a pair of bikini underwear. Don't French sailors *ever* wear clothes? In spite of him, or because of his girlfriend, we made it safely through and were moored in front of the Balboa Yacht Club by 3 p.m. after a very quick transit. We were in the Pacific!

By this time it was the end of June and very late to be making the crossing to the Marquesas Islands and beyond. But we wanted to reach New Zealand by November, and there were others still going (mostly French boats), so we thought we would be okay. We spent a week in Balboa, getting last-minute items, calling our children and generally readying TIGGER for a 15- to 35-day passage—15 if we stopped in the Galápagos Islands, 35 if we went directly to the Marquesas.

The Balboa Yacht Club was a world unto itself. It is gone now, burned to the ground in 1999, but it was the site of a mixed lot of humanity back then. Besides normal yachties like us (no really, we are normal), there were penniless vagabonds traveling the world in derelict boats; adventurers looking for a ride somewhere, anywhere; racing boat crews dashing from one transoceanic race to another. And of course, the "girls of the night," who arrived in the early evening and left with a new friend if the music, drinks and dollars were favorable. Though we were moored as far from the club as we could get, on Thursday and Sunday disco nights, the music sounded like it was on the next boat. It must have been earsplitting inside the club. One morning, I found them cleaning up after the night before. First they would sweep all the broken bottles and glasses in a pile. Then they took a hose and washed the beer, blood and possibly vomit, down a drain in the middle of the floor. Yuk! I wondered just what kind of party needed this type of cleanup. Come on Pacific, clean our nostrils and our ears!

7

Pacific Crossing—Take One

One windless morning we motored out through the ship channel and headed for the small island of Taboga, only a short distance from the Balboa Yacht Club. We intended to spend the night there in the anchorage, see a bit of the island and then start the passage the next day. The weather was benign and there hadn't been any wind for days, so we figured we would just motor through the Bay of Panama and catch the wind south and to the west.

The anchorage at Taboga was rough and uncomfortable, and my back was hurting, so we stayed on the boat all day. In fact, I would be plagued with low back pain, off and on, for the first two years of the trip. When it hurt, I would lie down and stay flat until it quit. Strangely, it never hurt when we were at sea.

The next day was bright and sunny, windless as expected, so off we went. As we got out into the Bay of Panama, a long swell from the southwest came up, a clue ignored. I was standing at the stern of the boat, holding onto the backstay and looking forward. As TIGGER slowly motored along, the swell would lift us high, roll along under us, and then down we would go until the next one. It was like a slow-motion roller coaster. The sun was shining golden on the ocean that day, and it reminded me of the rolling fields of wheat on a Kansas prairie.

By dark, we were farther out and on a more southerly course. The recommendation was to head south and only a bit west until the latitude of the Galápagos where we had decided to make a stop—then turn west and use the southeasterly trades that should be at that latitude. At the same time, however, we didn't want to get too close to southern Panama or the coast of Colombia because of the drug boats. They like to be left alone, and we wanted to cooperate in that department. Rumors were rampant about the drug business off the coast of Colombia. We weren't in Panama long enough to hear more than to stay away from the coast. All the drug stuff seemed unreal to me, but I didn't question the advice, just agreed it was a good idea.

When the wind finally did come several days later, it was out of the southwest. Great, it was supposed to be from the southeast. Now we were being pushed more southerly than we wanted and into an oncoming current. Soon we were sailing close-hauled into short choppy seas, heeling more than I like, and still not going in the right direction. We were heading more and more toward Colombia. Our first waypoint was to pass near Malpelo Rock about 360 miles southwest of Panama. But that course put the wind right on our nose. To make it worse, the weather had turned squally with lightning.

I hate lightning. I don't actually know all the consequences of a lightning strike on board a boat, but I have a great imagination and have always been pretty sure that if a bolt ever did hit us, it would blow out all our through-hull fittings, and we would sink like a stone. That at least was what had happened to a friend of Dave's—the boat had sunk almost immediately. Luckily, it was at a dock in seven feet of water at the time. But we were in much less friendly surroundings. So there we were, rail down, bashing into a headwind and current, and dodging lightning. I was not having fun.

How long would this go on? When would the wind shift? I knew we had to contend with the current for a while, but we were too close to Colombia, and if we tacked away from land we were going northwest. It was either Hawaii or Colombia, and we wanted the Galápagos!

I remember the day, it was all steel gray, and the sky held low clouds with lots of black on their undersides. The sea was choppy and rough, with only the white crests of the waves adding some contrast. Night came on the second day of the electrical storm, and it was very dark. I was seasick and un-comfortable. I just wanted to go home. I, who had lived and breathed a circumnavigation for the past four years, just wanted out. It was one hour into my watch. Dave was down below asleep when I woke him up. "Dave, I don't like this, I've had enough of the Pacific," I said. "I want to turn back."

"Huh?" was his first response, and then, "Are you sure?" was his second. He wasn't having any fun either.

In that moment, we changed TIGGER's course to a recipro-cal to head back to Panama, and I told myself I would never set a sea boot into the Pacific again. I had sailed in it, I didn't like it and I would have to be content with that. I never ques-tioned that it was the end of a dream. I forgot the fact that I was where I was supposed to be. It was as if I suddenly came to and said to myself, "What the hell am I doing here?" In that moment, I just wanted to be somewhere else.

Years later, re-reading my journals and the logbook, I was given a lesson in perception and memory. Since the turn-around, we had been telling people that the electrical storm went on for about four days. That at least was our recollection of it. It was never-ending, and we were just getting too beat up. What I read in the ship's log, however, was that the electrical storm had lasted less than 36 hours! I was shocked. It had seemed so long and we'd been so discouraged. I know now we were not mentally prepared to cross that ocean. I was home-sick and scared. Granted, I was fulfilling my dream, but those other feelings were the strongest at that time. I sure was surprised to find out how little it had taken to make us turn back.

Around midnight, when the realization of what I had done began to set in, I started crying. I knew then that I had made a terrible mistake. I wanted to turn around again, but Dave said, "No, we've made this decision, we'll stick by it. Maybe we can try again in February when the bulk of the cruisers go and the weather is better." I didn't believe we would ever try again, and I cried on and off for a lost dream all the way back to Panama.

Naturally, as soon as we turned back, we only had about five hours of tail winds and then the breeze turned to the northeast and we had a headwind again. Also, there was some kind of countercurrent, so we had the current against us again and were right back in the same damn miserable conditions. The electrical activity had passed, but it was a motorsail all the way back to Panama with me crying and Dave trying to console me.

I know the reason it didn't take Dave long to turn around was that he always wanted to please me. He had talked about a circumnavigation all of his life, but he would have given it up if I didn't want to go. He was determined to make me happy.

8

Patience Is a Virtue

Tucked alongside the Pedro Miguel Locks in the middle of the canal was a small boat club. It had been there many years, and although the buildings were old and rickety, the marina docks were safe enough. It had a small haulout facility and room for people to work on their boats if they wanted. It was away from both Panama City and Colón. It seemed the safest place to spend any amount of time in Panama. So we would have to go halfway back through the canal.

It was a paperwork mess checking back into Panama, since we had checked out and had not entered another country before checking back in. But with the help of a friendly agent and a $20 bill, we got back in, and just possibly, it was even legal.

Going through the locks this time, we tied to a tug. Then the tug was tied to the side wall. We had heard some horror stories about that kind of transit, but it was perfect. The tug was new and clean, and the crew professional. They took our lines, secured them well, and we rode steady as the lock filled. When it was time to untie, they did so quickly and let us get away from them first before they started moving. We went out behind them, but they kept their wake gentle.

Pedro Miguel Boat Club is about 100 yards to the side of the locks, and once all was secured we sat in TIGGER's cockpit and watched the cargo of the world go by, carried on the transiting freighters. We kept a booklet with pictures of all the flags of the world close at hand, so we could look up the flags whenever we needed to. There were rusty old Korean fishing boats, listing and creeping along with shark tails hanging from lines on the stern. We saw a nuclear submarine, with patrol boats around it so no one could get close, no-nonsense Japanese car carriers, looking like concrete city blocks with engines and a square-rigger training ship from Colombia. Even the stately QUEEN ELIZABETH 2, the largest ship to ever go through, was moved into place with only inches to spare. Day and night, they passed through the locks, crossing from one ocean to another. With a little imagination, it became a place of high adventure and romance. These ships were seeing the world. Hey, wait a minute, so were we!

Once TIGGER was settled we flew home again. Then we spent three months cruising the country in an old RV, visiting family and generally waiting out the Panamanian rainy season and getting mentally prepared to tackle the Pacific again. How do you mentally prepare? Luckily, like sailors everywhere, I had already forgotten the misery and fear, and we talked about the journey as if it were a foregone conclusion. Before, I was so afraid we wouldn't go, and Dave didn't say much. This time we accepted it as fact. We bought more boat stuff—radar, a computer for weather fax, and a million other items that we thought would help us remain self-sufficient so far from home.

Arriving back in Panama on Thanksgiving Day meant we had two months to do all the things we wanted to do to TIGGER and still head out in early February. Two things stand out in my mind about the stay at Pedro Miguel, the geese and the crocodiles.

The geese were Toulouse geese, a breed apparently known for its meanness. They were "watch geese" and meaner than any Doberman, discouraging even the people who lived there from entering. Every time I left the boat, the geese were harassing me. And they would bite if you didn't keep a very watchful eye and something handy to swipe at them with. One day I was just fed up; one was chasing me, and I turned around and kicked at him. I hit him in the head with the side of my shoe. And I'm not ashamed to say it was a good solid hit. He stepped back, shook his head several times like a boxer who's taken too many punches and staggered away. It didn't stop him from chasing me the next time, but that day I dusted my hands off with satisfaction.

Which brings me to the crocodiles. They were in the canal and would sun themselves on rocks around the marina. One afternoon we saw one that was nearly 5 feet long and I decided to take some pictures of it. As we were creeping closer for a good shot, Kris, the dockmaster, walked by and commented, "Hey, I wouldn't get too close, did you know they can run faster than a horse?" I gingerly backed away and took long shots of it. Later, the head-kicked goose disappeared and the general suspicion was that the croc had gotten her. I had a hard time feeling bad until her mate came crying to all the boats, honking and pecking, looking for his loved one. He even tried romancing a mooring buoy in an effort to get back that old feeling. Management felt sorry for him and got him a new partner, so I was right back where I started.

Often when the big ships came through, they needed a canal tug to help position them so the mules could take their lines and pull them in place within the lock. These tugs were very powerful with skilled operators who could move a 700-foot freighter just inches if need be to fit it into the lock.

Because of the way the marina sits adjacent to the canal, the tugs would often be perpendicular to some of the marina slips. If you happened to be in those slips, the wash from the huge engines on the tugs could really play havoc with the dock lines and cleats. We had a yacht protecting us from the worst for a while, but when it left, we were fully exposed to the prop wash of these tugs. Most of the time, Dave or I would get their attention, they would turn just a little, and the wash would pass by the slips at an oblique angle with no problems.

But one night we got the worst as a tug was positioning a big freighter—full blast and prolonged. Dave tried to call Canal Control on the VHF radio. He blew our air horn and flashed our spotlight. No response. All the while, the wash was pounding TIGGER's side putting a tremendous pressure on the lines. We had six other yachts "downstream" of us and if our lines or cleats gave way, we would be pushed into these yachts and it would be chaos. So these folks were on the dock with us trying to get the tug's attention. All of a sudden, we saw a flare go off behind us. It sailed up, up, over the tug and the big freighter, and into the jungle beyond. Hey, the tug shifted his angle! That was great. The wash went away, and we all went to bed, satisfied that whoever shot the flare had a good idea.

A few weeks later, I was talking to a fellow cruiser who had friends working in the control tower of our particular lock. I was telling her about that rude tug driver and our rescuer. When I was done, Barbara said, "Oh, so that's what happened." Surprised, I asked, "You knew about it?" Then she told me the rest of the story. Her friends in the control tower had told her about some crazy yachties who had shot a flare at a ship loaded with explosives. They only transit hazardous cargo at night. We knew that, but had been so worried about the wash we hadn't really looked at the ship. Barbara said when the flare was shot off, everyone in the tower just froze and held their breath while the flare went over the ship and not on it. They only started breathing again when it had landed safely in the jungle. We had a few nervous laughs about that one. Fortunately we didn't have any more trouble with prop washes so there was no further need for flares or signals.

During our earlier trip to the United States, we had missed buying a few supplies, so we had another shipment sent down to Panama, including a new staysail and several pieces of expensive hardware. This being Panama, we were anxious to get it, and get it intact and undamaged. So when the air freight office called the marina to tell us the box had arrived we went directly over to pick it up, even though it was a $50 taxi ride to and from the airport. When we got there and began to clear customs, one of the officials asked for a $20 "special duty fee," an obvious attempt at *mordida*, literally "putting the bite on someone." We refused to pay. After all, the box was clearly marked "yacht in transit," no duty required. It was our right to receive it duty free. I firmly protested, "No duty, no money, no, no, no."

The officer, however, chose not to understand English that day and spoke to another official in Spanish. The second officer apologized in English for the inconvenience, and then explained that the money was for the paperwork.

"No, no," I said with Dave backing me up all the way, "No duty or paperwork fees required." This was, after all, about principle, not the money. We had to uphold the fight against corruption, rampant in that part of the world. Still, he had our package and we wanted it. And we had money and he wanted that—a Panamanian standoff. Just when we thought our principles would hold up, the translator told us that if we wouldn't pay the $20, we would need a special waiver. That paperwork had to be done at another building, which would require another taxi ride and would cost $50. Damn! Our principles were crumbling fast, I said, "Okay, $20 it is." But the customs official was mad now, and he was going for nothing less than $50.

Off we went, steaming, in the taxi to a building across the airport grounds, where we got the paperwork. When Dave asked for a receipt, the official refused to give us one. Finally we got the paperwork, they got our money, and we got our box. Riding home we were so indignant we were practically foaming at the mouth. But in the end, I was starting to laugh at the whole crazy episode.

January in Panama is beastly hot, and we thought that, since we had a little time left, we ought to see a bit more of the country. With our friends Dolores and Bob on SUMMER WIND,

we rented a car and drove north to find some cooler tempera-
tures. We had heard there are actually mountains in Panama.
It was a delightful trip. We drove north to the city of David,
then east into the cool highlands where we found a most beautiful area near the Costa Rican border.

We stayed in a small hotel in Volcan and the next day
hired José, a local man, to take us in his four-wheel drive taxi
to Los Quetzales Resort. Located high up in the cloud forest,
as these misty mountaintops are called, we wanted to see some
quetzals, the colorful, long-tailed birds, whose shimmering
feathers were once used to decorate the elaborate costumes of
the Mayans. Today the birds are almost extinct, but there are
still some to be found in the truly remote regions of Central
America. So along a steep and deeply rutted dirt path we
bounced up, up by the Guaymi Indian caretaker's home and
into the clouds that perpetually cling to these hillsides.

The resort consists of a pair of two-story rustic cabins, with
a veranda circling each cabin, set in the middle of an astoundingly beautiful rainforest. Hummingbirds by the hundreds flitted around the cabins, feeding on the flowers. But we
missed the quetzals since it was the middle of the day, and they
only came back to nest around sundown. Still we enjoyed the
cool, beautiful setting and the solitude of the clouds.

We spent several more days in the mountains, driving
around this lovely area where the people cultivate both flowers and coffee. Then finally, we headed back down the mountains and within several hours were back in the hot Panama
we'd known before. I could have spent another month in the
cool, peaceful north, but it was time to set our minds to the
west. Time to tackle the Pacific again.

9

Tragedy Strikes

Before we could do that, however, we had to go back through the canal to Balboa. First Dave and I helped our friends on SUMMER WIND through, then we all took the bus back to the boat club and they helped us through. Again, we were to tie up to a tug, which was tied to the side wall. It had worked well last time, so we were feeling pretty confident as we motored toward the lock. The wind was about 22 knots behind us, and there was a current running, which was also carrying us quickly to the lock.

Since we were down-locking, TIGGER would be at the forward end, right at the gate, and the big ships would be behind her. All we had to do was drive up next to the tug, throw our lines to the crew, and they would secure us. As we approached, however, it was apparent we were moving too fast, thanks to the wind and current. Bob was to throw the bow line first, then I would throw the stern line. No problem, the lines would stop us and Dave could also put TIGGER in reverse. Unfortunately that's not quite how things worked out. My throwing arm failed me. Bob got his line to the crew on the bow just fine. But I threw my line short, and it fell into the water.

Now we were being pushed toward the gate, with a drop of

30 feet or so just beyond. The bow was held fast by the tug and acting as a pivot point, with TIGGER like the end of the "whip" in that game skaters sometimes play. TIGGER swung around and soon we were facing the opposite direction! The language barrier was all too evident as we shouted to the tug crew to let the bow line go even as they tried to haul in more line so that we would stay close to them. I saw our stern getting closer and closer to the gate and started saying some serious prayers. And by the time the crew finally let the line go, TIGGER's stern was only a few feet away. I broke into a cold sweat. Dave poured on the power to our 40-horsepower engine and never was TIGGER so eager to move forward as we finally cleared the area and lined up again for another try at the tug. By this time, however, my nerves were shot, and I asked Bob to throw the line at the stern while I took care of things in the bow. He did, and I did, and all went well. It was only after we were safe and secure that we noticed the 200 or so Japanese tourists watching from the observation deck of the control building. We acted casual—that's the way it's supposed to be done.

We were in Balboa, provisioning and getting mail, when the yacht LAMBDA NU left for Costa Rica, along with our friends on SUMMER WIND. They were sailing up to Costa Rica and then north to the United States. They had heard of the beautiful island of Coiba, off the coast of northern Panama, and planned to stop there. It was a national park and reported to be very spectacular. However, part of the island was a penal colony. I don't know if they knew that when they anchored, but there had never been any word of trouble, so we would have stopped there too, if it had been on our path. That night four men escaped from the penal colony and boarded LAMBDA NU. In the ensuing struggle, the skipper, Bob, was killed with his own gun. The convicts forced his wife, Vickie, to take the yacht to the mainland, where they made their escape. SUMMER WIND was anchored very close by, but they didn't hear a thing and were unaware of any trouble until the next morning when they saw their friends gone. They immediately knew that something was amiss and got on the radio, by which time Vickie had already gotten rid of the escapees and was calling for help. As we tuned in the morning radio net, we discovered the horrible news. We didn't know Bob and Vickie well, just as passing acquaintances, but I learned then that the cruising community is like a family, tied together by more bonds than many blood relatives.

Eventually Vickie managed to get LAMBDA NU to a small harbor, where a United States Army helicopter picked her up along with her husband's body and carried them back to Balboa. But there was more trouble. The next morning, local Panamanian officials arrived at the yacht and prepared to tow it away. The yachties on other boats in the bay were very concerned that the boat would disappear, or arrive at the police dock stripped of everything of value. It was a legitimate concern. One fellow jumped on LAMBDA NU, not letting the officials take the boat without him. Another brought out his camcorder to record what was happening. Another started calling on the radio for help from someone with authority over the local police. We followed all this on the SSB radio as it unfolded, and it was chilling and worrisome, and we were helpless to assist. This was not the 5 o'clock news, impersonal and unreal. This was happening to one of us. We all breathed easier when a call to the Panamanians towing the boat, from someone apparently important enough, caused them to cut the towing line. They took off in their towboat, and left LAMBDA NU drifting. Luckily, the sailor who stayed on the boat was able to get it back to safety. The yacht was safe, but Bob was still dead.

Everyone rallied around Vickie, and her yacht was taken back to Balboa by friends and then delivered to Florida. They had been a young couple on a great adventure. All sailors worry about the harshness of the sea, but that day we were reminded one more time that man is the harshest tool of fate by far.

10

⤶

Pacific Crossing—Take Two

The Las Perlas Islands were our first stop before making the crossing to the Galápagos. These lightly settled islands are in the Bay of Panama, stretching out into the Pacific, and although there were rumors that marijuana was grown and harvested there, for the most part whenever we'd visited we'd found only peace and quiet.

One time though, anchored off the coast of one of the smaller islands, we had watched quietly as a small boat with a big outboard came to shore, and several men stalked off into the jungle carrying gunny sacks and machetes. Gathering coconuts? I think not. An hour later they came back, sacks full, and it didn't look like coconuts. We stayed low in the cockpit and peered through the lifelines. They acted like we weren't there, and we reciprocated. That was the only time we saw that sort of activity.

We spent our last week in Panama among those lovely islands, relaxing, getting the bustle of Panama City out of our systems and getting TIGGER secured for the 850 miles to the Galápagos. We anchored off Isla Contadora, Isla Chapera and finally Isla San José. We had heard that Isla San José, the last island before open water, had a good fresh water stream to fill tanks and maybe do some laundry. Perfect, because we needed the week to recover from our start.

We had left the Balboa Yacht Club anchorage early in the morning, motoring out the ship channel, staying out of the way of what seemed especially heavy shipping traffic. Dave went down below to make a cup of tea while I steered and kept watch. Suddenly I heard a yell! Dave staggered up the companionway holding his face in his hands. "I'm burned," he cried. He had primed the alcohol stove by feeding it some alcohol and letting it burn off to heat the burner. But somehow, it had burned out and the alcohol had just kept leaking onto the stove. When he came back to light it again, he didn't notice all the alcohol until it exploded in flames in his face. I could smell the singed hair and see flames down below, but I couldn't leave the wheel, as a big ship was right behind us. I called out for Dave to get the fire blanket that was handy, right below the companionway steps, ready for just such a happening. But ever optimistic Dave wanted to let it burn itself out. He took his hands away from his face, and though his face was red, his skin didn't look burned. His eyes were streaming tears, but he said he could see again.

I was not so optimistic about the fire, and when he said he could see, I had him grab the wheel and went below and threw the blanket on the flames. Those fire blankets work great! The fire was out, and all was well again. However, when I checked Dave, he looked like one of those characters in cartoons who have a stick of dynamite blow up in their face; he had no eyebrows or eyelashes, and the front of his hair was little burned sticks standing out in all directions. The still smoldering fire blanket got tossed in the cockpit, and Dave stepped on a hot spot in his bare feet. He hopped around the cockpit, trying to cool his toes. I thought it was time for me to get back behind the wheel, dodging freighters where it was safe.

Isla San José has a good anchorage near the fresh water stream with a huge rock marking the entrance. It had been described by various people as a crouching monkey, a bust of

Calvin Coolidge or an Easter Island tiki. As we rounded it and entered the anchorage, we found four of our friends already anchored and waiting for the right time to leave.

A German couple, Dieter and Gerta, lived on the island and had a small garden and sometimes sold fresh vegetables to passing yachts. The morning after we arrived, Dieter came out to TIGGER in a dilapidated little dinghy, rowing with oars that had been a couple of two-by-fours only that morning. I judged his age to be in the mid-70s, and he had a pistol strapped to his side. He asked us our names, where we were from and our ages. He said he was the caretaker of the anchorage and since there had been trouble the previous year (a yacht anchored nearby had been boarded and the skipper shot), he was keeping an eye on things. He offered to sell us some pamplemousses, the grapefruit-like fruit found in Polynesia. We declined, not realizing that it is the most delicious fruit in the world. Don't ever say no to pamplemousse if it is offered. We heard gunshots in the night, but the other yachties told us it was Dieter shooting at crocodiles.

Woody and Kathy on WELKIN warned us to watch for a big crocodile when we went to the stream since he liked fresh water too. As we landed the dinghy we saw a deep trail in the sand with footprints on each side of it. This was no baby. I wanted to do the laundry and swim in the little pool and collect some fresh water. But it was hard doing laundry while looking over your shoulder watching for that lurking reptile. It was the fastest wash, swim and water collection I'd ever done. One thought went through my mind again and again. A croc can run faster than a horse. In the end, I dumped the fresh water. If crocs swim in it, I didn't want to drink it.

After three days of waiting for wind, all the boats sailed out early one morning, heading toward a common waypoint near Malpelo Rock so we would be going in the same general direction. I don't know why we bothered, because we always immediately spread out to give ourselves lots of sea room. We did, however, meet on the radio each day and before we reached the Galápagos, there were seven more yachts on the net. Yachts ahead of us and yachts behind us; there were a lot of us crossing in 1995.

What a difference this trip was compared to the last try— no wind, smooth seas and endless sunny days. This time the question was, "Do we have enough fuel to power 850 miles?" The answer was yes, because we had loaded 10 five-gallon jugs on deck for this notoriously windless leg. We carry 50 gallons of diesel in our tank, and with the extra fuel, we had 100 gallons. We powered almost the whole way, driving ourselves crazy with the noise and arriving in Admiralty Bay with about three teaspoons left in the tank.

As darkness descended that first day, so did fog— thick, heavy and wet. Here we were, still in the north-south shipping lanes, with zero visibility. Dave had installed radar on TIGGER for just this occasion, but I hadn't come to trust it yet. I strained to catch sight of any vessel barreling through the night, about to run us down. It was an exercise in futility, as I couldn't even see the bow of the boat. But I did it anyway.

Motoring through this black, black night, with the seas so flat, it was not all scary and dreary. For as we moved through the water, we stirred up phosphorescence, which created a halo of eerie green around TIGGER. There were also pale green sparks flashing on and off as the sea creatures were disturbed and then rested. Deeper in the water, the green glow persisted, so that the surface consisted of twinkling sequins against a background of shimmering, silver-green lamé. The churning propeller created a comet effect, and trailing behind us through the fog, I could see a long sparkling tail, diffused and softened by the mist. This strange and almost ghostly sight would either make your hair stand on end, or put you in a state of awe. I was experiencing a little of both.

I had a habit of sitting in the companionway for my watch, so I could see forward, and yet put on headphones and listen to the BBC on the radio or taped music without too much trouble. This same night, I was sitting quietly when I felt something fall past me, brushing my face, my arm and then my leg. I gave a little yelp and reached for the flashlight. I had the sensation that it was black and my first thought was that it was a bat. I know, a bat at sea, but there you go, bats scare the be-jesus out of me so that was my first thought. When I shined the light around the cabin sole, it turned out to be a little storm petrel. He apparently had hit the mast or a shroud, been stunned and fallen down. I picked him up and put him on the cockpit seat. He weighed no more than a feather or two, which he was. The little bird stayed there for a minute and then started fluttering. I was afraid he would fall off the seat and be in worse shape, so I put him on the side deck. He stayed there for a few minutes, not even blinking as I shined the light on him. I let him rest, and when I turned the light on a few min-utes later, he was gone. I hope he flew away and didn't just wander off the deck. In the morning, the fog lifted, revealing a cloudless sky, but still no wind.

The days went by, as we were motoring most of the time, drift-ing sometimes to seek a little peace from the engine sounds, and listening to the radio net and other cruisers who had wind in their sails. We took the advice of the experts and stayed east of the others, heading south first to find the southeast trades. Those who went against the norm and went farther west got northeast winds. Go figure. But we stuck with it, as Herb, the normally very accurate weather guru on SSB, kept assuring us that we were going the right way.

One day we felt a soft but steady breeze from the north and out came the dreaded spinnaker. It was an old sail Dave had kept from his days racing TIGGER at the Mentor Harbor Yacht Club in Cleveland, Ohio, with a crew of five. I'm here to tell you, a racing spinnaker is too much for a crew of two. Or, if there are only two, they need to be two under-30, testosterone-charged gorillas. My only experience with the spinnaker was my first time offshore when we sailed TIGGER from Florida to Houston. The wind came up suddenly, and we didn't get the sail down fast enough. Dave gave me explicit directions on how to help him get it down, but still we broached the boat and Dave ended up injuring his hand saving TIGGER from further disaster. We had to sail to Mobile, Alabama for medical care and ended up taking the Intracoastal Waterway most of the remaining miles to Houston.

I hated that sail, but we were desperate to turn off the engine, and in a weak moment, I let Dave talk me into flying it. It took about one hour to set it up. Then one minute to hoist it and get one of the lines from the spinnaker sleeve caught on the roller furling bearing at the top of the forestay while the other lines wrapped themselves around various lower shrouds. After that it took another two hours to unwrap the mess and get it back down. That night I wrote in my journal: "*Is flying a spinnaker grounds for divorce in Texas? We have only flown it two times in our married life, and today I actually threatened Dave that if he flew it again, I was leaving him in the Galápagos and going back to Houston. Okay, what I really want to do is throw the damn thing overboard.*"

Our watch schedule also changed on this leg. When we'd started out, we'd decided on three hours on and three hours off since we couldn't think of anything better. But this schedule had never been fully satisfactory as neither of us ever got enough uninterrupted sleep, and we would inevitably arrive in port exhausted and grouchy. While in Panama, I read Jim Moore's book, *By Way of the Wind* in which he writes that his wife, Molly, who liked to stay up late, would stand watch from 6 p.m. until she was too tired, usually around midnight, while he, an early riser, would then stand watch to the early morning, usually around 6 o'clock.

That seemed to fit our own sleep patterns so I took the 6 p.m. to midnight, and Dave took the midnight to 6 a.m., while during the day it was three hours on and three hours off. That way, we knew we would have at least five hours of good, uninterrupted sleep in every 24-hour period. There were exceptions, of course, but they were rare. It worked well, and we enjoyed our long passages at last. I was always looking for ways to amuse myself during the long six-hour night watch. I had books, music and the SSB radio to keep me company. I developed a nice routine that was only broken during poor weather when there were other things to do. First I would read until it was too dark. Then I would listen to a CD, or tune in the BBC, Radio Albania, or Voice of America. That I could hear a person speaking Albanian-accented English—and heavily accented English at that—from the SSB radio on our little boat in the middle of an ocean on the opposite side of the world is still a source of wonder to me. Then there were the heavens to look at and ponder, the sea to watch in the darkness, and dolphins to search for as they went zooming by leaving a trail of supernatural phosphorescence. I think I saw this once, and it kept me searching night after night.

Just before midnight, I would put hot water on to heat for Dave's tea when he took over. Dave drank Russian tea all night long. I doubt they drink this in Russia, but that's what it's called and he loves it. It consists of a mixture of a 1-pound, 2-ounce jar of Tang, ½ cup instant tea, 1½ cups sugar, 1 teaspoon allspice, 1 teaspoon cinnamon, 1 teaspoon ground cloves. Mix together and store in an airtight container. For each cup of hot water, use 2 teaspoons of mix.

The time had also come to throw off our clothes and sail au naturel. Why bother with clothes? They just got dirty and then needed to be washed. It was also much cooler now that we were in the tropics. Alas, but that day we tangled with the spinnaker, we paid for our freedom by getting burned in places that had not seen the sun in some time—maybe ever—and we couldn't sit without wincing for several days.

We were getting close to crossing the equator and wanted to make it during daylight so we would both be awake for a celebration. We were traveling roughly southwest now, still motoring, and had about eight miles to go at 4 o'clock one afternoon. If we kept going southwest, we would cross while Dave had his off-watch, so we changed course and headed due south. Shortly thereafter we became official shellbacks by crossing the equator at 82 degrees, 52.7 minutes west longitude. We had a small ceremony and gave a toast to Neptune. I wore a foil crown and held a scepter made from a dish scrubber. Dave wore a toga made from an old sheet, and we took a few pictures. Taking a picture of the GPS just as it rolled over to 00 degrees, 00.000 minutes latitude was not easy, but I caught it for history—all great fun. Then it was time for Dave to sleep and me to take the evening watch.

That night, I saw the sun and the full moon at the same time in a spectacular display. The ocean is perhaps the best place you can see this because of the unobstructed horizons. Usually when the sun sets, the sky is darker in the east. Or when the moon comes up, the sky is darker in the west. But that night the sky was bright on both horizons with the sun an orange, fiery ball sinking in the west and the moon a cool, pale yellow orb rising from the eastern waves—surreal and beautiful in this supposedly desolate desert of water.

There were so many unusual sunrises and sunsets. The colors were always different, more intense and vivid. Each day's show outdid the preceding one. The setting sun hurled streaks of gold and salmon and crimson, with filmy sundogs dramatic across the sky. The rising sun came up in a magnificent display, lighting the back of clouds on the eastern horizon with red and gold. All sunsets and sunrises were breathtaking and bold and full of glory. That was different from other oceans, where often the sunsets were soft and serene. Not here, in the eastern Pacific. Each day's beginning and end was nothing but power, grace and beauty.

11

✑

Hello Galápagos!

We spotted the islands as the sun came up on the thirteenth morning. Isla San Cristóbal, one of the easternmost islands, loomed before us. Obviously, we weren't going to be able to make the 80 or so miles to Isla Santa Cruz before dark. And our rule then was no landfalls in darkness. Even though the wind had come up as we neared the islands, and the current was carrying us quickly in the right direction, we would just have to stand off the island and arrive the following day.

Now I was nervous. I get that way after being off soundings for a long time. Our depthsounder records depths up to 300 feet and deeper than that will show just a dash instead of numbers. Even when the new depth is 200 feet, I clench up. It is like reverse velocity to me. You know—when you go 70 miles an hour for a long time, 50 feels very slow. Well, when you are in 20,000 feet of water for a long time, 200 feels very shallow. Dave says, "We only need six feet." I say, " TIGGER may need that, but I need a lot more!"

I wanted to sail far south and then come in between San Cristóbal and Santa Cruz and just heave-to between the two islands keeping well away from shores and shallow water. But

Dave had other ideas. First, he thought cutting close to San Cristóbal was just fine, and that using the freshening wind for a fun sail was great, like Sunday sailors having a good romp. We spent a lot of time that day in a brisk debate about getting too close to shore and heeling too much. At one point he stated, "We'll do what I say, after all, I am the captain." And he wasn't kidding! That didn't sit well, but it shut me up for awhile.

By evening, the wind had softened, and we were slowly sailing north between the two islands. At dawn, we would turn back south along the coast of Santa Cruz and hopefully enter Academy Bay, where we'd planned to anchor, around noon.

During the night, Dave was sitting in the cockpit as we quietly ghosted along under a bright moon, when he heard first one cough, and then a second or two later, another. His hair stood on end since I was asleep, and he was the only one in the cockpit. Or was he? He heard the sound again, and then a barking sound and some splashing. He shined the flashlight over the side to see several sea lions following the boat. Their coughing sounds just like a human being's.

In the morning sunshine, we started back south toward Academy Bay at the far end of Isla Santa Cruz. Following the coastline, we watched sea turtles and birds come to investigate the new arrivals. And of course, the sleek and friendly sea lions made their appearance, too. It very much reminded me of neighbors coming to check out the family moving into the house across the street.

Academy Bay was crowded with yachts that had come from Panama, Costa Rica and Mexico the same time we did. Next to our group were the local tourist boats, motor vessels that hired out to take visitors from Ecuador to the other islands. You needed a special permit to take your private yacht to the outer islands, and though we had applied for one over a year before and made numerous phone calls, we never received it.

The charges for entering the Galápagos at Academy Bay were pretty flexible. It seemed to change depending on who was the port captain at the time you entered and how much time you asked for. We asked for 30 days and got 10, which cost $170. Others paid more, some less. In fact, the yachts that came in several days later paid nothing because the port captain was rotated back to Ecuador, and there was no replacement for several weeks—no way to check-in, no fees.

Ten days gave us plenty of time to explore this amazing place. We took a minibus tour of the island along with a dozen people from the yachts in the harbor. The guide was a naturalist from Ecuador, a young woman who obviously loved the island and knew much about the flora and fauna. Santa Cruz is a fairly dry island, with lots of scrub and cacti. But there were some parts of the island that had rolling pastureland and healthy looking cattle. We went to the highest point for a breathtaking view of the waters surrounding Santa Cruz and the adjacent islands.

Next, we bounced over a dirt road to a lava tunnel, which had been formed when the outer shell of a long-ago lava flow had cooled and hardened while the inner core stayed hot enough to continue moving until the flow finally petered out leaving a tunnel. This one was about half a mile long, 10 feet high and 20 to 30 feet across in most places. We entered the tunnel by climbing down a hole in the ground. It was dark and damp, with lush fern growth all around the entry, and a sleepy barn owl roosting in among the ferns.

I am a bit claustrophobic, but with my flashlight on I was doing fine until the middle. Suddenly my chest got tight and the walls started closing in. I couldn't see the opening at either end. Whew! It took some good conversations with myself to keep from knocking everyone down, and stumbling my way either forward or back, toward an opening. But then I calmed down again and enjoyed the rest of the walk; lots of stalactites and stalagmites, with the water dripping from the ceiling still forming these "mineral-cicles."

Later, we chanced upon several giant tortoises. Two different pairs, well over 100 years old, were in the process of mating in a farmer's meadow among the scrub trees and shrubs. The males were mounted on the females and, although we observed them for over an hour, they remained in that position! The guide cautioned us to be very quiet as they were easily stressed by people and noise and thus would not complete their mating. I don't think there was a problem; they managed to stay unstressed the whole time we were walking around taking pictures. We could hear the "ouff, ouff" of the males as we drove away.

Then since Dave and I are birdwatchers, the guide took the group to an old volcanic crater, where she said there were plenty of vermilion flycatchers. As we tramped through the scrub trees, in a drizzly rain, I was thrilled to see three of them, but Dave was always looking the other way. Later a Darwin's finch followed him for quite a ways, flitting from tree to tree as Dave made "finch" sounds. One of the other cruisers commented that birdwatchers must be crazy, but we knew that already so we didn't take offense.

On another day, we took our dinghy out to a small island in the bay, which was home to a large colony of sea lions. They saw us coming and soon there were heads popping up all around us. The water was too deep to anchor, so I stayed in the dinghy while Dave jumped over the side to swim with the sea lions, who dove and twirled and careened around him. The water was cold so he didn't last long. And my swim was even shorter. One sea lion took a deep dive and then zoomed up from the bottom, which was too deep for me to see, and practically bumped into me on his way up! I screamed into my snorkel, and he turned and looked at me and, I swear, laughed before he took off again. By then, I was blue. The waters here on the equator are surprisingly cold because of the Humboldt Current, which comes up from Antarctica, so we called it a day.

The 3,018 miles to the Marquesas Islands made our next passage the longest we had faced so far, and we were anxious about it. But we'd heard about the steady southeast trades and the exotic Marquesas, so after our allotted 10 days, it was time to go.

We had anchored in the bay in front of a large steel power-yacht and had both a bow and stern anchor set, so we would not swing as the wind shifted. It was just too crowded in the anchorage to swing freely, and all the yachts were anchored in this manner. Even though we were in a mere 20 feet of water, we couldn't see the bottom, and when I pulled on the stern anchor line, I got some resistance. I took a turn around the winch in the cockpit and cranked. With a "crack" the line parted. One end missed my face by inches, and the other dropped back into the water. I managed to grab the end in the water before it sank. But I had no way to haul up the anchor. And when a swell came, I lost the end of the line.

We were bemoaning the loss of a $200 anchor (even worse than the cost was the fact that we couldn't replace it out here) when Dave decided to try at least one dive to see if he could locate it. "I'll give it one shot, but I doubt I will find it," he said, and donned his mask and fins. Diving under, however, he immediately saw the end of the line—it had not sunk to the bottom yet—and followed it down. Then he located the anchor! Somehow, our stern anchor line, which was rope as opposed to chain, had gotten under the poweryacht's bow anchor chain, where it had chafed for 10 days, so that the strain we put on it hauling it up had caused the parting. The line was also tangled in his anchor and chain near the bottom. Down Dave went again, and in three quick, neat dives, he untangled everything. I attached another line to the frayed end, and we winched up the anchor. Now it really was time to go.

12

❧

Naked at the Helm

We sailed out of Academy Bay with two other yachts in late March. The good southeast trades were there, and the seas were light. But once out of the protection of the islands, the sea set up a pattern that was to last for the next 3,000 miles, one of an infernal rolling. Whether the wind was strong or the wind was light, the rolling never stopped. It was like a special kind of torture, and several times I had to pause, take a deep breath and recite a mantra or two to keep from screaming. Later, in those conditions, I *would* scream just to relieve the built-up tension.

For days the winds remained steady from the east and southeast, and our course was anywhere from west to west-southwest, depending on where we found less uncomfortable rolling. We were never actually comfortable, but some points of sail were better than others. The boats ahead of us reported squally conditions, but we missed them. We were making 140 to 165 miles a day, with an accommodating current that runs west from the Galápagos almost to the Marquesas.

A few yachts stopped at Isla Fernandina, the westernmost island in the Galápagos, and home to an active volcano. But since it entailed getting off our rhumbline course, and since our hearts and minds were now on the Marquesas, we gave it a miss, even though our friends reported a spectacular fire show.

The night watches were always a bit tense for me. I didn't like the dark, and I was forever dreaming up scenarios where we would have an emergency, and I couldn't see what was wrong because of the darkness. On the SSB radio net one day, a fellow cruiser asked me if I knew the stars of the Southern Hemisphere. I didn't and that night, I made it my business to begin learning the names of as many as I could. I got out our copy of *Dutton's Navigation and Piloting*, turned to the sky chart of the Southern Hemisphere, and spent my moonless watch learning their names. After that night, when my watch came and the sky darkened and the stars would appear one by one, I viewed a more familiar heaven. I would say, "Hello, Orion, there you are. And you Procyon, and now Pollux and Castor. I see you Capella, and there's Pleiades and Aldebaran and Bellatrix and Rigel. Hello friends, I knew I could count on you." Then I would settle down for a more comfortable watch.

One evening I wrote in my journal: " *Tonight, I looked at the sky and went in and got my copy of* The Rubaiyat of Omar Khayyam.

> And that inverted Bowl they call the sky.
> Whereunder crawling coop'd we live and die,
> Lift not your Hands to it for help—for it
> as Impotently moves as you or I.

It has been over 35 years since I first read that verse, when I was a junior in high school. I was probably the only one of Miss Ericson's students really taken with them, but to me they held all the exotic mysteries of the world, all the romance and adventure that the Old Tent-Maker could conjure up. There are those critics who say he was a lousy, maudlin poet, but I love him if only for the way he put words into images for me. I can truly see the caravanserai camped out on the Persian desert, under the "inverted Bowl they call the sky"—as black as this night. And then our little rolling, rocking, uncomfortable ride takes on the romance and adventure I had hoped and dreamed it would be."

I had bought a stalk of bananas, small and very sweet, for the long trip to the Marquesas, and hung them in the cockpit. The trick was to keep them from all ripening at the same time. That's very hard to do. But one suggestion was to cover them, and they would ripen slower. What did I have to cover them with? I found a man's shirt I had bought to cover me from the sun and buttoned it around the stalk. Perfect, it fit just right. Except one night I came up from down below and forgot about the bananas and saw a headless man's torso swinging gently in the moonlight. I almost fainted. The bananas ripened all at the same time anyway, and we each ate up to 10 bananas a day for a while.

April Fools Day! I called Dave out of a sleep to see a non-existent whale. I tried to feel guilty, I really did, but I was too busy laughing. He had already played a few tricks on me earlier that morning.

Later, when I yelled, "Water, there's water coming in!" he thought it was another joke. But I guess the fear in my voice got through to him. I had lifted the floorboard because I thought I'd smelled bleach and found that the water was up to the top of the bilge and spilling onto the cabin sole. I flipped on the electric bilge pump, then began madly pumping the manual one in the cockpit. Dave, still half asleep, started hunting the source of the influx. After a few minutes, it was clear we were getting ahead of it, and we calmed down a little. Then I remembered he had been in "Hell" earlier that day.

Hell is our storage area under the cockpit. It is cramped and hot if the engine has been running, and you have to be a pretzel to get to anything anyway. Sure enough, when he had been in Hell, he had accidentally knocked loose an intake line for the watermaker, letting a small but persistent flow into the bilge. There'd been no hose clamp. It had been a temporary fix about a year before, and totally forgotten. Once again we were reminded that no mistakes can ever be forgotten on a sailboat. Sooner or later they remind you. It was an easy fix, but the high water in the bilge had shorted out a connection on the radar, and it didn't work again until we had it repaired in Tahiti.

For two weeks we laid a zigzag course south and west to try to be comfortable. We had no need to search for wind or current; they were always there. One morning we shook a reef out of the main and heard that dreaded sound: "Rrrrrrripppp!" The main had ripped its full length on the seam at the first reef.

Even though we were pretty sick about it, the sail had raced and cruised for 20 years, so there was no shame in its giving up the ghost. After trying to hand-stitch a repair, I came to the conclusion we would have to fly a double-reefed main to the Marquesas, where I could get the machine out and do some repairs. That night on the radio net, another Dave on the yacht RUBAIYAT reported that he had just shredded his jib. Plans were hatched to order new sails from New Zealand, have them shipped together and save some money. So we met our new Lidgard full-batten mainsail in Papeete, Tahiti.

Each day there would be another inch to add across our large-scale chart of the Pacific. Like an ant crossing a football field, the progress was slow if you took the whole ocean at one glance; the ocean was so wide and we were so small. Still, each day there would be another inch or so to plot on that chart marking our progress to landfall. We were moving west and land was just over the horizon. How very satisfying that was—and is—to me.

Even though we were naked most of the time, there were still a few items that needed to be washed, so I decided to try using the rocking of the boat to wash them the way I had once read it could be done. I had bought a five-gallon trash bucket with a lid in the Galápagos, which I now filled with water and soap. I put dirty clothes in it, put the lid on and lashed it in the cockpit. We certainly had enough rocking to keep it agitating. After about six days, I opened the bucket to take out my clean, just-like-a-washing-machine clothes, and instead found a thick layer of algae and scum, staining those items nearest the top. From then on the bucket was for washing, with me the agitator.

As the third week began, the current slowed down and so did the wind. We still had the rolling, but we weren't moving as fast as we had at the beginning of the passage. There's that reverse velocity theory again. We were down to 130 miles a day, then 120 and then one day only 80. That was when the damn spinnaker came out again. And it's not a spinnaker: It's a *damn* spinnaker. Don't doubt me on that one!

In fact, we were flying the damn spinnaker the day we came closer to sinking than at any time on the whole trip, one of only two times in our journey I really thought, "This is it." The other time was later down the line. But this day was sunny, very clear with light winds, the spinnaker up and a little less rolling than usual. Dave was below napping, and I had just finished the lunch dishes. I had been down below about eight minutes. Normally, if I had chores down below, I would pop my head out every six to eight minutes, take a quick scan of the horizon, and then finish the chores. I had read books by other circumnavigators who took it easy in the wide expanses of the open ocean; some even slept all night. We never got that comfortable, but did feel that in the middle of nowhere— that is in the middle of 64 million square miles of Pacific Ocean—our chances of hitting another boat were pretty minimal. So I took my horizon scans and felt safe.

That day, I mindlessly came up, sat in the companionway and was looking forward at the set of the spinnaker when I heard a noise. It sounded like an engine. Was there a plane overhead? I looked up in the sky. No, I didn't see a plane. Then I heard it suddenly louder, and I turned to look toward the starboard side. Good God! A ship was right there, about 100 yards from us, coming up from behind on the starboard quarter, and moving fast! I screamed for Dave, jumped to the wheel, turned it hard to port and started the engine at the same time. Luckily, we had enough speed with the spinnaker up that TIGGER turned well, and the ship, a black-hulled freighter about 700 feet long, skimmed past, missing us by about 75 feet. Dave rushed on deck to see this behemoth just as the bow wake started rocking TIGGER like a toy boat in a stirred-up bathtub. As it went by, I looked up and saw a man on the bow. He had a broom in his hand and was just standing there looking at me. He was the only person I saw. When Dave realized they had safely missed us, he rushed to the VHF radio and hailed the ship, which brought several people on deck, all with binoculars, looking at a plump, naked grandma with terror in her eyes!

Though the ship was of Greek registry, the person who answered the call sounded Japanese. He spoke good English. Dave asked him, "Didn't you see us?" He answered, "No, so sorry." Dave said, "Didn't you have a watch?" The man politely answered, "No, so sorry." Dave was exasperated.

"Didn't you have your radar on?"

"No, so sorry, do you need anything?"

Dave asked me, "Do we need anything?"

"Yes," I shouted. "We need them to get out of our ocean!" They were going so fast that they were a speck on the horizon in 15 minutes and gone in 20.

We have thought and talked about that episode many times since it happened. There we were, out in the middle of nowhere, on a clear sunny day, with a huge colorful sail up and we had nearly been rammed. They just plain weren't looking, except for the man on the bow. And I wonder if he would have ever said anything if they actually had hit and sunk us. He couldn't have warned the bridge. He was 600 feet forward, and the ship wouldn't have felt even a twinge as it mowed us down and we went to the bottom.

The most chilling aspect of this episode was that no one else would ever have known what had happened. The radio net had heard from us that morning. But if we didn't check in at night they would have said "radio problems" as we were already pretty weak on the frequency they had chosen. They'd have thought no more about it, and it would have been a long time before anyone worried. Then there was that big ocean—

no, it was too horrifying to contemplate for long, and while we talked about the experience itself, we didn't talk much about how it could have turned out.

Then again what about my own responsibility in this instance? Right you are to ask. As much at fault as the ship was, I was equally at fault. It was my watch. I was below for the most part and not vigilant enough. In way of explanation, I think when I was scanning the horizon the ship was coming up at an angle that was behind the dodger. But she was moving so fast, that I probably only missed seeing her once before she was on us. Bottom line though, I was derelict in my duty.

Both Dave and I learned a most valuable lesson that stood us well in the next three years. We always had someone on deck. If it was our watch, then that is where we were—on deck, watching. We stayed on deck during squalls, gales, hove-to, and on clear sunny days. We no longer had a casual attitude about these big oceans and all that room. When I went to the head while Dave was asleep, I was nervous and hurried. When I made tea on my watch, I was nervous and hurried. I could only relax when on deck because I knew this time no ship could sneak up on me!

As it turned out our paranoia was justified. The very next afternoon another ship came at us on a collision course. This time we saw it and took evasive action. They obviously didn't see us, and we called but got no answer. So the lesson was reinforced immediately and set a new pattern for the rest of the circumnavigation.

It was also at this time, just when we really needed it, that the reacher-drifter, an easy-to-handle lightweight headsail, ripped at the top. I managed to hand sew the tear, so it stayed together for the last few days. But a permanent fix was beyond my ability. Luckily, we found our friends Bridget and Rob on MIDGBIL at anchor in Hiva Oa, and they did a fine job repairing sails, so we were able to press on with not only a sturdy reacher-drifter, but a full mainsail as well.

13

❧

The South Seas at Last

The morning the island of Hiva Oa materialized on the western horizon, I shouted, "Land ho!" with as much gusto as any of the salts of old. I still get choked up when I shout that age-old call, following the traditions of the sea. Twenty-three days at sea and this little island, eight miles by 40 miles was right where Dave's sextant and Uncle Sam's satellites said it would be. What must it have been like for the early explorers who didn't even know if there would be land? It feels right to shout, "Land ho" for them as well. Later, sailing along the south coast of Hiva Oa we flew the French courtesy flag, and Dave sang the French national anthem, "La Marseillaise."

It was late afternoon as we turned into the little bay. I looked behind us and a complete rainbow framed the view from the stern. Forward, five dolphins frolicked in our bow wake, welcoming us to this beautiful island and leading us into the anchorage. I was here at last, my heart's home, Polynesia.

If there was a down side to our landfall, it was that the bay was not meant for the 30 or so boats that were anchored there. So it was bow and stern anchors again, as we all rested up before spreading out to explore the islands of French Polynesia and other points west. The bay was about one mile long and perhaps a quarter mile wide. It was surrounded by high, craggy hills, covered with all shades of lush green. On one hillside there was a small French army garrison, and each evening, its songs would carry across the anchorage as the men marched to dinner.

At the far end of the anchorage, the hills formed a V shape that created a perfect framework for Ursa Major, the Big Dipper and the other brilliant diamonds against the velvety night sky.

After the long spell of just sea and sky, I was overwhelmed by the beauty of the island. I had lived many years in Hawaii, and was already in love with the myriad soft shades of green, the vivid pinks and purples, and the other riotous colors of the tropics. My eyes and heart were filled with the colors, and I inhaled the fragrances until I was dizzy. This island is Paul Gauguin's final resting place; he also saw the colors and spent his life capturing it all on canvas.

An immediate visit to town was in order along with some food—something different, and lots of it. I did a minor swoon when I entered the small grocery store and saw olives, pickles, chips, Cokes, cookies, and my beloved chocolate—the joyful, fun foods of Americans. I did a major swoon when I saw the prices. When I left the store, just a little light-headed, I had one jar of olives, one bag of chips, a dozen eggs, two pieces of meat and several cheeses, and a candy bar. The bill was the equivalent of $78! At least the baguettes and French cheeses were cheap. We feasted daily on these items until we were sick of them.

Each day we walked the mile or so to town, calling out "bonjour" to the smiling Marquesans. They, of course, called "bonjour" back, although their bonjour sounded nothing like our bonjour. I guess it had something to do with the accent.

One day Bridget and Rod and Dave and I hiked to some petroglyphs on the side of one of the steep hills. The lime trees grew wild there, and though all the land belonged to someone, the limes on the ground were understood to be okay to pick up and take back. The best fruit of all is the kind that you can pick in the forest, sort of like the Garden of Eden. Well, at least these weren't apples.

There was a young couple who came around in the afternoon selling local fruits, oranges, pamplemousses and bananas. The first day, the young woman asked if I had any earrings. I ran down below and got two pairs of "trading earrings" I had brought along and told her to choose which she liked best.

"Oh Madame," she cried in her lovely French accent, "I just love earrings!" For the pair she chose I got six extra oranges.

We had heard so much about the beauty of the island of Fatu Hiva that, 12 days later, we decided to beat into the southeasterlies for a visit. We had also heard they were shrewd traders. I hadn't brought a lot to trade, but had a few little trinkets of the kind that had worked well in Hiva Oa. The men who came to the boat to trade, however, were only interested in power tools, Sony Walkmans and cassette tapes of Van Halen. We wouldn't part with our power tools and didn't have the other two items. So for about 60 feet of good line, several pairs of earrings and some canned goods, we got six pamplemousses and a mango.

The day we left, another yacht in the anchorage lost their dinghy, when the dinghy painter frayed, and it drifted out to sea. Since they were leaving that day anyway, they just took off, heading out with the current, hoping to find it. We said we'd keep our eyes out for it as we headed north, although there was little hope of spotting anything in such a very big ocean. Four hours later, however, they called us on the VHF radio to report they had found the dinghy, bounding along, drifting with the current, about six miles west of Fatu Hiva. What are the odds, I ask you? Amazing.

Gradually we made our way north to Nuku Hiva, stopping at spots that looked inviting. But generally, the anchorages were not snug and well protected from the swells, and we were disappointed after 3,000 miles of rolling to be rolling again!

On the way to Nuku Hiva, I caught my biggest fish of the

whole trip. I had been trolling with little success since Panama, but since I had caught quite a few dorado in the Bay of Panama, I was determined to keep trying. Fishing was a new endeavor for me and even though I am opposed to killing any living creature, except for a few select insects, the taste of fresh fish helped me set aside any philosophical qualms. The 40-pound wahoo took my lure just as I was pulling in the line one afternoon while sailing along the coast of Tahuata.

My fishing line consisted of a piece of wood, on which I wound about 200 feet of 80-pound test line, and a yellow feather lure. The dorados in Panama loved that lure, and so apparently did the wahoo. I wrestled with that fish for a while, and finally got him to the boat, where Dave had the net waiting. Our secret to killing fish quickly, without having a bloody mess, was to pour alcohol in their gills. Gin was the best, but Dave protected his gin ruthlessly, so any alcohol would do. Since we were on our way to a popular anchorage, I had a fish

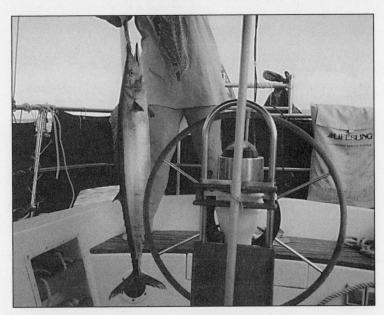

The 40-pound wahoo caught my lure, Tahuata, Marquesas

Taiohae Bay, Nuku Hiva, Marquesas

story to tell and the fish steaks to prove it. Quite a few boats dined on wahoo that night.

Taiohae Bay on Nuku Hiva is huge, a horseshoe-shaped bay whose waters gently wash against sandy beaches in places and crash noisily on volcanic boulders in others. Unfortunately it was also rough although we were becoming resigned to that by now. This time, the bow and stern anchor were both out to keep TIGGER facing the swells that rolled in the mouth of the bay. At least the yachts were spread out across the bay, so no one needed to worry about elbowroom.

Once we were settled we took a tour with several other couples from the anchorage over the mountain to the north side of the island. There are very few roads on Nuku Hiva and this was not one of them. In fact it was a small goat path, rutted and filled with rocks and even boulders that our guide Jean

Paul had to find ways to get around. The island is volcanic, steep and rugged. Two of our tour mates were Karen and Earl from SPIRIT WIND. Later, SPIRIT WIND would sink on the way back to Vancouver, British Columbia. Luckily, a navy ship was nearby at the time of their distress call. They were in their life raft less than 12 hours. I guess they don't call that lucky, but then again, maybe they do.

We spent several weeks at Nuku Hiva, enjoying lunches at the Keikahanui Inn where Rose Corser was the owner. She was off the island while we were there, so Jean Marie was the fellow we depended on for food and for phone calls that needed a French translation. Jean Marie was a Peter Lorre look-alike, perfectly typecast for the part of the world-weary, cynical French expatriate. Every time I saw him, the music from "Casablanca" started playing in my head.

After a short stop at the island of Ua Pou, a day's sail from Nuku Hiva, we set sail for the Tuamotus. This group of islands was once called the "Dangerous Archipelago." Its islands stretch almost 1,000 miles across the Pacific from the northwest to the southeast. The islands are all coral atolls; low, sandy dots on the face of the vast ocean. Before the advent of GPS, most cruisers gave them a miss, and we would have too since knowing your position only once or twice a day among all those low atolls would have been too scary. Although it was a clear day we had to sail to within six miles of Takaroa, our first landfall in the group, before we could actually see the island.

Even with GPS, we couldn't really trust the accuracy of our charts for this part of the ocean, since we used whatever charts we could scrounge, and some of them were copies of copies, with the last data collected over 100 years ago. Of course, the position of the islands hasn't changed in 100 years. But the method of calculating longitude and latitude has, so these charts could, and sometimes did, misrepresent an atoll's position.

An atoll is like a necklace; a circular ridge of coral, most of it still underwater, with small islands rising above the surface like pearls on a string. Most of the atolls have only one or two channels deep enough for a sailboat to enter the lagoon. And you generally need to enter at the end of an incoming tide, preferably at slack high water, when the water is neither rushing in nor rushing out, since the currents through the narrow openings can be swift and dangerous. At Takaroa, you are required to stop at the dock just inside the entrance, for clearance to proceed farther into the lagoon, since they do a lot of pearl farming. The harbormaster then tells yachts where to anchor. We were greeted by two fellows from the weather service office on the island, and also by Luigi, an Italian crewmember from the small sailboat docked in front of us.

We ended up staying at the dock for three days because the weather changed and with the cloudy weather, coral heads are harder to see. To reach the place where we could anchor, we would be crossing the whole lagoon, full of coral heads. So we sat tight and waited for the sun and the right tidal situation again.

The little village next to the dock had about 50 people, a small grocery store, a church and a bakery. The bakery was a mile or so out of town on a crushed coral road lined with palm trees. We walked out one day, but I guess you have to be there at 6 o'clock, as it was closed when we got there at 10 a.m. No fresh bread for us. Also, when the supply ship from Papeete is late and there is no flour, they close up until the supply ship arrives.

Louise, an islander, came to visit the first day and welcomed us to the island. We had heard they were always short of bananas on these atolls, so we had brought some with us from Nuku Hiva. I gave her a bunch and she invited us to visit her home. We walked up the path to her house the next day. When we arrived, she was weaving pandanus hats for us and gave us each a shell lei. Her husband, Henri, had diabetes and gout, so he was sitting in the main room, with his feet up. They didn't speak much English but were hospitable and generous, and we enjoyed our time with them.

There were little chicks running around the living room. They pecked at my bare feet while the rest of the family watched *In the Heat of the Night,* a cop show from America on a 32-inch color television! I was astounded. First, they had three televisions, as well as an electric keyboard and a boom box. Second, they were watching a violent American program and probably thought that's the way life really is in the United States. Thirdly, each of these islands—even those with only 50 people—had a receiver of some sort to pick up the TV stations that broadcast from Tahiti, hundreds of miles away.

As it turned out, only one television worked; the rest of the electronics were broken in some way. Dave looked at them to see if he could effect a repair, but finally had to admit there was nothing he could do. Later, we were told that the Tuamotuans receive a stipend from the French government, and since they have little to spend cash on, they order expensive electronics, no doubt having seen them on TV. It seemed a bizarre situation to me, living in paradise and watching misery-laden television shows from America.

The dock had a small copra shed set on it and that first night I heard the sound of small feet scrambling on deck, which I thought was a dog since there had been several very mangy looking animals hanging around during the day. The second night I heard it again, and when I got up in the morning, I found rat droppings on deck. That was it! We were closing up at night! Dave then admitted that the first morning when he got up there had been rat droppings on the cabin sole at the head of our V-berth which he had cleaned up before I woke up. I asked Luigi, our neighbor, if they were having trouble with rats, since they had already been there for 18 days. He said no, he had only seen the rats on the dock by the copra shed. I wonder why they loved TIGGER so much? When we saw Luigi again in Papeete he told me that when they finally left Takaroa and raised the mainsail, three big rats had jumped out of the flaked sail! Luckily, our rats didn't stay on board. Still I was glad when we could pull our docklines in and motor into the lagoon and anchor away from land.

We spent two serene weeks in the lagoon, mostly alone,

never going to shore, and only leaving the boat twice a day to snorkel. We were anchored close to two spectacular coral patches, and it was a 20-yard swim to our own aquarium. One night I wrote in my journal: *"Fantastic sight! It is a warm night and the moon is almost full. The wind is about 20 knots, with small wispy clouds flying across the sky. Just now, Dave was on the fore-deck checking the anchor, when he called me out. There, near the boat, was a white ghostly form, slowly gliding below the surface of the water. It would surface, then dive, and then surface again. It was huge, about 14 feet across. Then, just for a second, I made out its mouth and wings. It was a manta ray, so big, and yet graceful as a ballet dancer in the moonlight. As it made wide, sweeping curves, gathering food, it would summersault, showing first its white underbelly, and then its velvety brown topside."*

That vision has stuck firmly in my mind, mysterious and beautiful.

Another night when the moon was full, I went on deck looking for our ghostly visitor. The water was so clear and the moon so bright, the water "disappeared" and the sandy bottom of the lagoon and the coral appeared with perfect clarity. TIG-GER was sitting 20 feet above, seemingly suspended in midair.

Coming out of Takaroa's lagoon was easier than going in, since we didn't have to stop at the entrance and could ride the out-going tide. A German yacht had come in several days earlier, and we'd visited back and forth those last days. They were leaving the same day we were, so Dave and I decided to wait until they'd left, and then follow them out. That way, if they had any trouble, we would see it and be warned.

The channel going in and out was a dogleg, with two sharp turns. Once you were on your way there was no turning back. Being swept along by the swift current in a channel only 50 feet wide didn't leave much margin for error.

The ideal time to enter the channel that day was at 2 p.m., but while we patiently waited for our friends to leave, they hung around so long we thought maybe they had changed their minds, and we went ahead instead. Surprise! As we entered the channel they were right behind us. Apparently they'd had the same idea about letting someone else go first, those rascals. We caught the current, maneuvered the corners, and hung on while the swift waters spit us out into the ocean again.

Toau, 97 miles west of Takaroa, is different from the other atolls in that it does not have a navigable opening. The anchorage was actually a little cove on the outside of the lagoon, a future entry passage that had not yet broken through the last of the coral. It was a lovely place with only one other yacht anchored nearby. Again, we spent our days snorkeling.

Here the reef fish were huge; it was like swimming in an aquarium on steroids. The clown fish, the damsels and the butterfly fish were all twice the size we were used to. We swam among 40-pound groupers and several black tip sharks. One especially strange fish had stripes across his eyeballs that matched perfectly with the skin around his eyes. Even though there was some old coral damage, perhaps from a cyclone that had hit many years earlier, the coral was mainly healthy and colorful. There were huge coral heads covered with Christmas tree coral, the little tube worms that swirl out of their tube to look like a Christmas tree, catch bits of food drifting by, then pop back in at the slightest sense of danger. They were every color imaginable—think of a big box of crayons—all shades of reds, yellows and blues. We would snorkel until we were cold, get out and have hot chocolate and rest; then it was back in again until we were chilled. Those were our days in the Tuamotus, and I remember them as the most idyllic of the whole journey.

14

The Society Islands

After a short, rough, 223-mile ride, I spotted the peaks of Tahiti at dusk the second day, still 80 miles away. It took us almost 24 more hours to get to the anchorage because of a fickle wind, then no wind, then headwinds. But at last, we sailed into Papeete Harbor—one of Dave's long-held dreams—and anchored in the "low rent district," where it was Mediterranean-style mooring with an anchor off the bow and a long stern line tied to shore. This area is further away from the main part of town than the more expensive area whose amenities included a seawall to tie to and even shore power. But you had to pay for those luxuries.

It was late June, and we were planning on spending Bastille Day in Papeete and enjoying the festivities. However, it was a year of political unrest since the French had announced plans to test a nuclear bomb in the southern Tuamotus. This seemed a cue for the independence movement to take action again, with protest marches and many festivities either cancelled or postponed. Still, Papeete was a fascinating place; the big city after the quiet of the other islands. And then there was that French character. Even out here in the middle of the Pacific, they had it. While I'm not necessarily a

Anchor out
forward,
line to shore,
Papeete Harbor,
Tahiti

Francophile, I readily admit they have style. Panache, élan—
it's that certain something, and it's very attractive.

Then there's the market place in Papeete. Where else
would you see a 250-pound, muscle-bound Tahitian man, tat-
toos covering half his body, with long flowing black hair and a
delicate flower behind his ear? Or a mahu (transvestite),
dressed in a lovely formfitting red sequin dress with a black hat
and veil squeezing the produce at 9 a.m.? Large banks of colorful flowers were for sale next to rows and rows of vegetables,
some of which I recognized, some of which I didn't.

Giving up on Papeete for Bastille Day, we headed for the
beautiful island of Moorea, and spent 10 peaceful days anchored in Cook's Bay, then Oponohu Bay. I took picture after
picture of Shark's Tooth Peak, in every possible cloud-peak
combination, because each one looked too beautiful to pass up

and better than the last. There was also more snorkeling, and more socializing. After the long spells of solitude while out on passage it was good to see our friends again. We hadn't seen some of the yachts since Panama, so there were a lot of stories to swap.

Earlier that year, before we'd left Panama, I'd gotten the wonderful news that my oldest daughter was pregnant again. But the distressing part was that it would be a high-risk pregnancy since, when her first baby was born, they had forgotten to give her the shot that makes the Rh factor not a problem and so now it was a problem. I told her then to take care of herself and the baby, and I would be home by the time the baby was born. With this in mind, we decided to put the boat on the hard on the island of Raiatea, northwest of Moorea, and catch a ferry back to Papeete and fly home. Our new grandchild was due in August, so we started toward Raiatea to get TIGGER ready for a six-week hiatus.

Sailing between islands in the Societies was always rough. The winds were brisk, and the seas lumpy and uncomfortable. We stopped at Huahine, a particularly beautiful spot, and stayed there for a week before sailing across to Raiatea, just 20 miles away. While in Huahine, we met some fellow Texans off a cruise ship who were sightseeing on the island. It was always fun meeting nonsailors, because they thought we were so adventurous. It made me feel special, and it helped me forget that I had been seasick the whole 90 miles from Moorea.

After that came the busy time of getting TIGGER out of the water and on supports at the Raiatea Carenage. After which we took the famed Ono-Ono ferry to Papeete, which we quickly renamed the "Oh no, Oh no" ferry because the ride was so rough, we couldn't stay in our seats. Imagine riding the mechanical bull at a Texas fair—that's what it was like as the hydrofoil hit the 4- to 6-foot waves at a speed of 25 knots. A young girl in the seat next to me threw up much of the way, without the benefit of an airsick bag. There were paper towels strewn about the floor to cover the mishap, because no one could clean it up without being thrown around themselves. It took seven hours to get to Papeete. The airplane ride back—we didn't make that mistake twice even though the ferry was half the price—was about 40 minutes.

In the end, however, all was well, and Grandma and Grandpa made it back to Texas in plenty of time to welcome a sweet and healthy baby boy into our family and into the world.

15

Southbound to the Cooks

Six weeks was long enough to be away from TIGGER, so we hightailed it back to Tahiti in mid-September. It was a shock to arrive at the international airport in Papeete and find it severely damaged with the customs building completely destroyed by fire. Even the beautiful frangipani trees in the parking lot were burned down. Parts of the city had been looted and many shops ripped apart. In late August, the protests in Papeete had reached a fever pitch, and the result was this sad sight. Luckily, the worst had not reached Raiatea, so TIGGER was safe.

The plan now was to sail to Bora Bora, some 25 miles away, spend a week or two there and then head for Aitutaki, in the Southern Cook Islands. I had read all my life about exotic Bora Bora and now gazed at its peaks each day from our spot in Raiatea. With our boat stuff from the United States loaded and the Panama-purchased bottom paint rolled on, we headed out again, eventually anchoring just inside the reef on the western side of Bora Bora, in front of Toopua Island. The water was shallow all around, and we were anchored at least a half-mile from shore. There was a small *motu*, or islet, about a mile behind us on the reef.

One afternoon as I was puttering in the cockpit I saw a dog swimming to the boat. I couldn't figure out where he had come from since we were so far from land, but he looked like he was swimming from the small motu. I quickly grabbed the dinghy painter, ready to jump in the dinghy and effect a rescue. But he just veered away from the boat and headed for the shoreline off our bow. He appeared to be swimming strong, nose staying above the water, so I watched him through the binoculars to make sure he was okay. Eventually he got to shore and ran up to a fellow who had just landed a runabout on the beach. I never did figure out where that dog came from, but he must have covered at least a mile and a half. That dog could swim!

It was a time of high winds and squalls, with only an odd morning or afternoon of sunny weather, so after seven days we were off to Aitutaki, almost 500 miles to the southwest. We were now in the Intertropical Convergence Zone, an area of intense, unsettled weather, and we were not having fun. First, we had light winds from behind, which caused uncomfortable rolling. Then, when the wind shifted to the southeast, it picked up to 15, 25 and then 35 knots. All the while, the skies were overcast, with intermittent lightning and thundershowers.

I had never had to heave-to, so I asked Dave to show me how it was done since this seemed like it would be a great time to give it a try, and it would also take my mind off the misery and mal de mer. In 35 knots of wind, we hove-to and it was like getting off the roller coaster. The wind was still 35 knots, the rain was still pouring down, but the boat was quiet. Now I knew what all the books were talking about! TIGGER did quite nicely with just the reefed main, sheeted in tight, and the wheel hard over to windward and locked. She was forereaching, or moving forward at 1 knot or less. That one experience was worth all the lousy weather, because after that, we hove-to more and more often. It was easy, and it settled things down and gave our bodies and our nerves a rest when they needed it. Each time, we tried different sail combinations and when the chips were down and we really needed to heave-to, we usually just flew the storm trysail and that did a great job alone.

The entrance channel leading to the anchorage in front of the small village on the southwestern side of Aitutaki is narrow, winding and shallow, but after those last four days, I was ready to stop, no matter how winding or shallow the channel. We arrived in a squall, with very heavy showers and no visibility, so TIGGER paced back and forth near the entrance markers. Dave raised the Cook Island flag, and I shouted, "God Save the Queen!" several times until the squall passed, and then we carefully wound our way in. The anchorage was as small as reported, but we managed to drop the hook in eight feet of water with just enough swinging room to avoid a rocky breakwater.

Aitutaki is a tourist island, which surprised me, since it is so isolated. But there is a big airport there, and a lot of New Zealanders, Australians and even Europeans take their holidays here. A Swiss couple we met said that this was a stop on some around-the-world tours from Europe. Although the two

TIGGER at anchor, Aitutaki, Southern Cook Islands

resorts at the north end of the island were full, it didn't show at our end of the island, and we enjoyed the quiet, friendly village where everyone spoke English and greeted us with a smile.

Back in French Polynesia, I'd gotten the distinct impression that although we were not exactly unwelcome, the people would just as soon be left alone; possibly the result of the tensions over the nuclear testing or the language barrier. Whatever the reason Aitutaki was a delightful change.

One evening, we walked to a hotel for the Polynesian show, and Dave did his version of the Cook Islanders' interpretation of the Tahitian dance. He always seems to wind up on stage! The evening ended with some more contemporary dancing, and the first record they put on the turntable was George Strait's "All My Ex's Live in Texas." We let the younger people have their fun and walked back to the boat in the moonlight.

The next day we took a tour boat with the other tourists to several small islands on the outer reef. Since the lagoon is strewn with coral, it is not safe to take a yacht anywhere except the small anchorage. The boat driver took us across the lagoon, dodging coral heads at speeds that made me pale. But he knew the lagoon intimately and missed every one of them. One islet was a tropicbird nesting area. These tropicbirds have long thin red streamers for tails, and red beaks. They're white with black feet and a black eye mask, and are very striking and vivid. The islet was a sandy spit with only two low, but spreading, scrub trees. In one of the trees, low to the ground, we saw a baby bird with Mom, while Dad circled and swooped overhead, trying to distract us. It was thrilling to see them in their nesting area, but we were making them very nervous, so we quietly walked away.

The season was progressing and New Zealand was the goal, so soon afterward we headed out for Rarotonga, farther south in the Cooks. We had planned an early morning departure, but Dave got delayed with the harbormaster, and when he came back he suggested that since the tide situation was no longer optimal, we ought to wait until the next day. I, however, dug in my first-mate heels. I had already waited several days to leave. And high tide, low tide, or no tide, I was ready to go.

As we motored out the channel, the depthsounder read seven feet, then six feet, then—good grief—four and a half feet. Since TIGGER's draft is almost five feet, we were in trouble, and seconds later we skidded to a stop. It was sand, so no damage to the keel, but we were stuck, and no matter how we tried to power through, we didn't budge. It wasn't long before a helpful cruiser came zipping out in his dinghy with a 15-horsepower outboard to help us muscle our way through the sand. Soon we were off the little bar into seven feet of water again and on our way.

Rarotonga was only 140 miles south from Aitutaki, and since the winds were light southeasterlies, we motorsailed all the way to assure we would get there in daylight the next day. I was horribly seasick the whole way and spent my watches planning the little cottage and flower garden that I would have when we sold TIGGER in Rarotonga and flew back to the United States. This is something I routinely did when I was seasick as I needed the promise of a life without mal de mer to keep going. Of course, I cancelled those plans and gave TIGGER a kiss as soon as we got into the quiet waters of Avatiu Harbor.

Like at Papeete, we put out a bow anchor and then tied a line from the stern to shore, to keep from swinging. The harbor was small, and there were about 30 yachts waiting to head out for New Zealand. Five of these were part of the "Peace Flotilla" returning from Moruroa in the southern Tuamotus. They had sailed there to protest the nuclear testing and were now heading home.

Don Silk was the harbormaster. I'd heard that he had written a book about his experiences delivering cargo in the South Pacific for the past 30 years or so. The book is called *From Kauri Trees to Sunlit Seas* and is a rollicking sea story. I bought a copy, and both Dave and I had a good read.

There was one memorable party while we were there. It

was a gathering of New Zealanders, Australians, Americans and Canadians, with lots of stories about the flotilla's adventures. We already knew how much we liked Canadians—I don't think I've ever met a Canadian I didn't like—and that night we found out what a great bunch the Kiwis and Aussies are.

It was now late October and we still had 1,800 miles ahead of us. " Let's go," I courteously requested of Dave. See? I was trying.

16

&

Heading Down Under

We left Rarotonga with 15 knots of wind out of the south-east. Within six hours, the wind died and we motored off and on for the next five days, the winds either light or non-existent. Our first four day's runs were 120, 110, 90 and 79 miles. Then the wind returned, and we never had another windless day in the 18-day passage.

The third day out, the engine's seawater cooling pump started leaking thanks to a load of sand it had taken in while we were trying to power off the sand bar in Aitutaki. Apparently the sand had chewed up the impeller and the pump was now leaking. Dave replaced the impeller, but still it leaked. He tried several times to replace the gasket, but it kept leaking badly. Finally he decided to replace the whole thing but the spare pump also leaked, so he took the old electric sump pump from the shower and bypassed the faulty engine driven seawater pump. It took power to run, and he was concerned it would take more power than the alternator would produce by running the engine. But it didn't, and we found we could charge the batteries. That pump probably ran 60 hours on that passage, after which it was put back to work as a sump pump when we reached New Zealand. The sump pump was 18 years old, while the engine driven pump was only 2 years old.

The next thing to go was the autopilot. We'd had trouble with our new autopilot almost as soon as we'd left Galveston Bay, at the very beginning of the journey. Since we had two—one for spare—Dave switched control heads, but no dice. Then he changed the fluxgate compass. Still no dice. Finally he changed the new fluxgate so it would go with the old control head. Bingo, it was working again. Ultimately, we had them repaired in Panama, New Zealand and Australia, before finally throwing one of them away in Darwin. By that time we'd spent almost as much on repairs as we had to purchase them new.

After that it was the alternator regulator's turn to go. Dave bypassed the regulator and wired in a switch and a small light bulb for resistance in the field current. Then he could switch the field current off if it was charging too much. I didn't, and still don't, understand it all, but he did and kept a careful watch on battery conditions.

In the meantime, the weather had deteriorated as we moved farther south and west. We now had 20 to 25 knots of southeast wind most of the time, and our plan was to sail to a longitude just west of the north end of New Zealand. After which we would turn south and east again. That way, if a sudden westerly came through, as they often did at that latitude, we could still make it down the coast without beating into the wind. That, at least, was the advice of the experts. As we got closer to New Zealand, however, Dave said, "Forget that," and headed along the rhumbline for the north coast of New Zealand.

I had been calling Dave "Rhumbline Ragle" for quite some time, since he always started out with a sail-by-the-wind plan, but then reverted to a shortest-distance-between-two-points course whenever that plan required sailing off the rhumbline.

By this time, we were flying the storm trysail and using the jib as needed. Mostly, it was rolled up to just a handkerchief-size sail. We had added a midstay with a storm staysail while in Panama, but using it involved going forward to set it up, and actually, TIGGER did quite well using the jib or the trysail alone. At the end of our journey, we concluded that the midstay and staysail were probably a waste of money for us.

On the thirteenth day out, the wind shifted to the south. Now we were beating into a brisk headwind and made only 87 miles in that first 24-hour period. Finally, the wind picked up to 30 knots, still from the south, and we hove-to. Enough was enough.

That afternoon, hove-to, I was on deck when I saw my first whale. It was about a mile away, and at first I couldn't tell what it was because of the white foam blowing off the wave tops. Looking through the binoculars, however, I could see it was a humpback whale, which occasionally showed the white on the underside of its flipper as it rolled it out of the water. It must have been a huge whale, and I was nervous that it was there, even as I felt a sense of awe. I wanted to see whales, but at the same time I didn't. I had read about their hitting little yachts like ours, and I wasn't interested in setting out in a life raft in these seas, or any seas, for that matter.

That night, still hove-to, I sat out my watch in the cockpit, huddled behind the dodger, bundled in a sweatshirt, long pants and full foulweather gear. I saw a ship pass in the distance, the first one I had seen since Rarotonga 13 days earlier. We were 300 miles from the entrance to the river leading to Whangarei so I supposed we were in the New Zealand shipping lanes now and would start seeing more.

Eighteen hours later, the wind shifted more to the southeast, and we eased the trysail, rolled out just a hankie-size jib and started moving again.

When I spotted Cape Brett at 6:30 a.m. on the eighteenth day, I once again shouted, "Land ho!" And as we got closer to the coast, Dave raised the New Zealand flag and I saluted and cried, "Hail to Aotearoa, the Land of the Long White Cloud." We always tried to have a ceremony when raising the courtesy flag of any new country—just for fun. By the way, Aotearoa means "Land of the Long White Cloud" in Maori.

Trying to reach the customs dock 30 miles upriver, before night and overtime charges, we rushed past the acres of rolling dark-green velvet pastures dotted with fluffy white sheep grazing on the hillsides. The smell of the earth was overwhelming. After so many days at sea, the fragrance of the grass and trees and soil was pungent and powerful. It was a wonderful smell, of land and of life.

We arrived at the customs dock at 6 o'clock, Sunday night. We had gone to the consulate in Rarotonga and gotten the list of restricted items for entry into New Zealand, so we could be ready for the quarantine officials. Since their country is primarily agricultural, the New Zealanders are very particular about foreign agricultural products bringing in new diseases.

The customs dock is near the head of the river, and we rafted up to a Kiwi poweryacht. Graham, the skipper, helped us tie up and called over for us to come have "tea" with him. After the check-in, which was painless since we had nothing left on the boat in the way of restricted foods, we stepped over to Graham's boat, and enjoyed a steak dinner with our new acquaintance. Hmm, we are invited for tea and get a steak dinner. . .

"Welcome to New Zealand," he said. We indeed felt welcome.

Our stay in New Zealand started out sadly, as that was the year the yacht MELINDA LEE was hit by a freighter and sunk, killing three members of a family of four. Only Judith, the wife and mother, survived to tell the story. It seems they were about 30 miles off the entrance to the Bay of Islands, on the north coast of the North Island, with gale force winds blowing. In the early hours of the morning, a freighter hit the 47-foot yacht, sinking it in minutes. One child, Benjamin, went down with the yacht. The others, a young daughter Annie, Judith and Michael, her husband, managed to grab onto a half-inflated dinghy that had broken loose. The life raft had gone

down with the yacht. In the ensuing hours, Michael and
Annie were unable to stay with the dinghy and perished. After
about 40 hours in the water, Judith was washed ashore, severely injured. Since there was already a search out for them,
she was eventually rescued and taken to the hospital in
Whangarei.

Even years later my heart sorrows for Judith. The shock
was severe for the cruising community as a whole. These were
people we all knew and had traveled with for thousands of
miles. It was a hard time also because no one wanted to talk
about it for fear of starting rumors, or feeding the media's already voracious appetite. We let a local television crew interview Dave and I to tell of our earlier mishap with the freighter.
But I felt guilty and worried even as we did it. It is hard to heal
when you can't talk about a tragedy, and even more so when
speculation as to "who was to blame" is running rampant in
the cruising community and on the news. The sea can be a
cruel taskmaster, and though it was the sea that ultimately
took them, it was again man who was the source of the
tragedy.

During our five months in Whangarei and the Bay of Islands, we mostly worked on TIGGER. After 19 years and all
those rough miles, she needed a few updates and some tender
loving care. She is always loved, but we can't always be tender.
We replaced the alcohol stove with a propane one, bought a
new inflatable dinghy and outboard, installed a wind steering
unit, replaced old batteries, added extra handholds down
below, added more shelving in the galley and sewed new sail
covers. Sanding, painting, varnishing: We did it all.

I even learned how to preserve meat and canned 25 jars of
beef and chicken for the upcoming season when grocery stores
would be few and far between. A Canadian woman, Sharon on
the yacht MORNING STAR, showed me how to cook the meat,
pack it in sterile canning jars, pressure cook it like crazy, and
then cool and store it. Of course, this entailed standing in the
galley, with the flame on our new propane stove up high while

the summer heat poured down into the boat. I called my little corner, "Hell's Kitchen," and sweated the hours away—90 minutes pressure boiling for each batch of jars to be exact. You'd think boiling meat for 90 minutes would render it something other than yummy, but actually, it was quite good. And when no handy butcher shop was around the corner, I could reach into my larder and whip up something delicious.

Whangarei was a perfect place to do our work. The city marina is right in town and there are chandleries and repair facilities all within walking distance, as well as doctors, grocery stores, a library and two beautiful city parks. The people of New Zealand are some of the friendliest I've met, and it's a country of sailing fanatics. You would have to be a fanatic to sail in those wild waters.

We decided to take some time off from all our work to go on a backpacker's tour to Waitomo with its very odd glowworm caves and Rotorua, which has both geysers and mineral baths. What an experience; of the 50 people on the bus, we were the only ones over 24. And we are a long way over 24. It was great fun except for the loud music that was constantly being piped over the speakers whenever the bus was in motion. I can rock with the best of them, but not at those decibels. The international group of young people was friendly, interesting and polite, but they will all be deaf by the time they're 30.

We saw only a bit of the interior of New Zealand since sightseeing is expensive even when the exchange rate is favorable, and we had spent a lot of money working on TIGGER. Sometimes just living in a country can be more enlightening than sightseeing anyway.

As usual, the season and the weather made the final decisions as to when to leave. Try leaving earlier than nature dictates, and you risk getting pounded for your efforts. As it was, this was the second year after the "Queen's Birthday Storm" off the coast of New Zealand, in which seven boats were abandoned, 21 crew rescued, and three souls lost at sea. It's easy to get jittery about sailing from New Zealand, but it had to be done to keep moving on our journey around the world.

We had decided to join the Island Cruising Association, a great New Zealand organization that sponsors several regattas a year. This would give us a chance to stay with the Kiwis for a while and have a regatta experience on our trip through Tonga, Fiji, Vanuatu and New Caledonia. Around October, we would head for Australia to safely sit out the cyclone season once again.

It was with this in mind that we sailed up to Russell in the Bay of Islands, to prepare to depart New Zealand with the fleet early May, 1996. While we were waiting, we heard there were pippis in the next bay, small clams that live on gravelly beaches and are delicious to eat. We took the dinghy to the secluded beach, grabbed our bucket and went to a spot just above the tide line. When I brushed the small rocks aside, there they were. In fact, everywhere we uncovered the gravel we seemed to find more and more. It was like finding gold nuggets. We were ecstatic and ran around the beach, picking up pippis and keeping a lookout for any other cruisers who might have found out about our gold field. That afternoon we steamed the little guys in wine, dipped them in butter and feasted. There is something so childishly gleeful about finding free food. Like the limes in the jungle on Hiva Oa, nature seemed to hold out her hand and say, "Take." After that there were a few more trips to that beach. My mouth still waters when I think of those pippis.

17

❧

Excerpt from my Journal

May 13, 1996, Position 22 degrees, 09 minutes South, 176 degrees, 27 minutes West:

What a trip! Leaving the Bay of Islands, we sailed into a rough sea and cold southeast wind—25 to 30 knots—that stayed with us these seven days and is giving us a fast ride north toward Tonga. Those first few hours, we could see the tougher Kiwis and Aussies were flying full sails, and ahead of us and off to the sides the other 40 or so yachts were thrashing and crashing through the 10-foot waves. We lost them all after about six hours and have been alone on the ocean ever since. We had immediately reefed down, and most of the time we've used a double reefed main or the trysail, with a little bit of jib.

I have been seasick. Not incapacitated, just grumpy, and Dave has been happily cooking down below while I turn my nose to the wind so as not to smell the food. I am rather shocked to say I haven't washed my face for seven days or changed my underwear. And that's the good news. The fact that I brushed my teeth twice a day is part of the bad news. I brushed them to get the God-awful taste of seasickness out of my mouth, not that it did me any good.

We have also used the first few days to get the feel for our new wind steering unit. We purchased it used for about one-third the price of a new one. It's the German-made Wind Pilot. It has an auxiliary rudder. The wind blade directs the servo-oar, which directs the auxiliary rudder. TIGGER's main rudder gets locked in neutral or adjusted a small amount for weather helm. What a difference it has made to use the wind to steer us and not the mostly faulty and energy-guzzling autopilot. Hopefully, Willy will be able to steer us even in light winds. We've heard from friends that it may wander a bit, but that even when the wind is behind us, it should do the job. We shall see. So far, we like it.

We are now 300 miles south of Nuku'alofa, and the wind has shifted northeast and increased to 35 knots. Time to heave-to again—easy stuff now and welcome after seven days of leaping and crashing over 8- to 10-foot seas. I have cleaned the cabin and cooked a meal since my mal de mer has abated, and we are both getting some rest. One of us is always on watch, of course.

In these first seven days out of New Zealand, we haven't taken our foulweather gear off. That's why the underwear stayed put. The cold southeast wind comes right off Antarctica. We also have had the kerosene heater going for the first time since leaving Galveston. I've been wearing my underwear, then long johns, then a sweater and sweatpants, then a sweatshirt, and then the foulweather jacket and pants with a watch cap pulled tight over my ears. We've both been standing watch, eating and sleeping in the same layers. There is something very primitive about it all, and I imagine this is what hunters, who go out tramping in the woods, carrying guns, spitting and sitting in deer blinds must like. I've always thought it was a macho guy thing to get so grungy, but I kind of like it too. There's a

*certain sense of freedom not to be tied to a personal hygiene
schedule.*

Let me digress: I remember when I was a kid, about 5 years old
and we were visiting my grandparents' farm in Minnesota. The
whole family was going to town, and my sister, my little cousin,
and I all had our going-to-town clothes on. We begged to go
out to play while the grown-ups got ready. The last words we
heard as we ran for the door were, "Do not get dirty and do not
let your little cousin get dirty." Poor, innocent little Wanda
was only 3 years old, while my older, more responsible-and-
should-have-known-better sister, Lily, was 6.

Out we went and made straight for a mud puddle. We really didn't intend to get dirty, but there was the mud, and we
were drawn to it like moths to a flame, bees to honey— well,
you get the picture. I still remember the heady sense of freedom and joy I felt as I slung mud pies at my cousin and sister.
There was no holding back; my little 5-year-old soul simply
took flight. I was covered with mud, and so were Wanda and
Lily. It was glorious! It's an episode of my childhood that I
have remembered with fondness all my life. I imagine everyone has at least one of these experiences stored in their memory banks; they're worth keeping.

However, there did come a moment when my sister and I
realized what had just occurred and the possible consequences.
I could hear my mother calling us, and we all knew we were in
for it. I grabbed Wanda, and headed for home, prepared for the
spanking that was coming. My older and-should-have-known-
better-sister lagged behind, delaying the inevitable, and I
could hear her wailing and whining behind me on the path.

Many good things have happened since then, many moments of freedom and soaring. But for pure unfettered joy,
nothing matches that time on the farm with mud flying everywhere and my companions' laughter ringing across the fields.

I suppose that's why I could go seven days without changing clothes. But enough childhood memories. Back to the log.

When we hove-to I stripped down to change a few layers and they all could stand alone, so I ended up taking a refreshing sponge bath. The only used item that went back on was the foulweather gear, again.

We were 90 miles east of Minerva Reef when we hove-to. Minerva Reef rises from the depths of the open ocean, up to the surface where high tide covers it completely, and low tide uncovers just a small portion. It is an atoll, and it provides a protected anchoring spot in the middle of the vast waters between New Zealand and the islands north. Cruising yachts and fishing boats often stop there to rest on their way to and from New Zealand, but we chose not to, because reefs in the middle of nowhere scare us, and besides, we had no detailed charts. Still, as we sat hove-to, we were slowly drifting west towards the reef. Like a kid who likes to scare himself, Dave announced once an hour that we had moved one more nautical mile closer. After 30 hours and 30 miles of creeping toward Minerva Reef, however, the wind lightened and shifted southeast and we were once again off to Tonga.

18

The Kingdom of Tonga

It took 11 days for TIGGER to get to Atata Island, the first stop in Tonga; pretty good time, since we were hove-to for 30 hours of those 11 days. When we left New Zealand, all 40 sailboats were quickly lost to us, disappearing one by one over the horizon. Then, like magic, just a few hours before making landfall, sails started appearing again. When we entered the reef surrounding the island, five other boats were right beside us.

The festivities of the regatta began there, and for a week, there were parties and games and general mayhem. New Zealanders seem to love parties, and it showed in the sometimes juvenile, sometimes very clever activities. From Atata, we each went our separate ways and then gathered again a month later to sail from Tonga to Fiji, another leg of the regatta.

Tonga is divided into island groups. Nuku'alofa is the capital of Tonga, located in the south island group. Farther north is the middle group, the Ha'apai Group. Then to the north of that is the Vava'u Group, where there is a big fleet of charter boats. The Ha'apai Group has been the least visited in the past because it is poorly surveyed, and is littered with reefs, both charted and uncharted.

The Vava'u Group has the best charts, because the charter fleet has produced a chart book of its own, listing all the anchorages and their conditions. They are not referred to by their names—I guess the charter companies don't think their customers could pronounce the names—but by numbers. We purchased the guide, as did many other yachts, and throughout our time in the Vava'u Group, we all referred to anchorages as "that great No. 12", or "don't even bother with No. 3," or "I caught a fish when we were anchored in No. 5." We tried to break ourselves of that very bad habit—we were after all guests in a country that had anchorages with real names, but the number system had its advantages.

The waters in the Ha'apai Group were hellishly rough, with the islands far apart. But in the Vava'u Group, the islands were close together, the waters were mostly calm and the anchorages so lovely that it was no wonder the charter companies liked it so much.

There was a lot of socializing in the Vava'u Group, and we had picnics on secluded beaches and pizza parties in our cockpit. Each boat would bring something to put on a pizza, and someone would make a pile of pizza crusts. Then I would crank up the oven to 450 degrees Fahrenheit and sweat like crazy to make pizza after pizza to be consumed by the willing occupants of the cooler cockpit. I would finally come up red-faced and laughing, to consume the best pizza, the one I saved for myself!

For some reason, I was lonely and melancholy that cruising season, although I found a special friend in Joanna on the sloop MAEVA. Joanna and her husband, Andrew, were Canadians, and MAEVA was an old wooden boat, lovingly restored and beautiful. Joanna was a veterinarian and made it her mission to feed and water any animals she found on the more isolated islands. Compared to America, the care of animals in Tonga was appalling. Even the pigs were skinny. Andrew was an engineer, and he did lots of work for the villages they visited, fixing both things electronic and mechanical. Needless to say they were welcome wherever they anchored. With Joanna, I could be my old pessimistic self if I wanted to, and she would not only listen but add her own complaints, so that moments later we would both be laughing at how spoiled rotten we were. Even in a South Seas paradise that most people would sell their souls for, we could still find things to complain about! She would always perk me up, and I was lucky to find a friend who saw my less than charming side and still liked me.

The island of Hunga was dedicating a new church while we were in the Vava'u Group, and the residents kindly invited any yacht that wished to join them in their celebration. So we sailed to Hunga, entered the very narrow passage into the lagoon and anchored near the village where the church was located. Several other yachts sailed over too, and church dignitaries from Nuku'alofa, at the south end of the country, came to dedicate it. This was a great honor for so small an island. The dignitaries arrived in a small fishing boat, loaded to the gunwales. They had flown to Neafu, the only town in the Vava'u Group, and taken the fishing boat more than 20 miles to this island. How they managed to cross open water in that boat, loaded as it was, is a mystery to me.

The ceremonies were much like church dedications all over the world, except that the women were wearing long muumuus and the church leader, an elderly gentleman, wore a frock coat. The church elders were very dignified and took this as a solemn occasion, but they must have been sweltering, since they were in suits and ties. It was all in Tongan, so I don't know what was said, but still, it was quite a moving ceremony. After the dedication, they had a traditional Tongan feast laid out in a lean-to next to the church with mats on the ground for us to sit on, long pieces of wood for tables and banana leaves for a tablecloth. Every house in the village contributed dishes for the feast. First the guests and dignitaries ate, and since we were guests, we sat first. When the feast was done, they merely lifted the table, still loaded with food, and carried it like a stretcher around the village to distribute what was left. Roast pig, taro, poi, coconut dishes, rice noodles, spinach in coconut milk, hot dogs and the beloved corned beef. For some reason, the people of the South Pacific love corned beef, and wherever we went, cans of corned beef were a welcome gift.

On another side of the lagoon was a yachties' hangout called Club Hunga. Run by a New Zealander and his Tongan wife, they welcomed sailors and served drinks and sandwiches. They had a pet pig named Banana, who generally had the run of the place. He'd lost his mother as a baby and had been raised on bananas which he still loved. Banana was adopted by a missionary group in the United States, which sent $15 a month to feed him. This club, surrounded by palm trees and tropical flowers, and set on the edge of the lovely lagoon, was a true South Sea Island hideaway.

Normally, you are required to check out of the country at Neafu, but because we were part of the regatta, the officials from Neafu came over in a boat and checked us out of the country en masse. This saved all 40 boats from having to converge on Neafu at the same time and made for a nice touch at the end of our stay in this lovely country.

Dignitaries and guests eat first at traditional feast after church dedication, Hunga Island, Tonga

19

❧

Busted! Is Honesty
Really the Best Policy?

The regatta had also made arrangements for checking in to Fiji at Savu Savu, but this didn't go quite as smoothly. At the time Savu Savu was not yet an official entry port, and while the government was preparing it to serve that purpose, it wasn't quite ready, so only some of the required officials were in place, and there was lots of confusion.

This situation was further complicated by the fact that we had alcohol on board. Dave had stocked up on his beloved rum before leaving New Zealand because of the high cost of liquor in the islands. The question, of course, had been whether to declare it and pay an exorbitant duty, or not declare it and hope that we didn't get caught and possibly pay an even more exorbitant fine if we did. In fact, both these options could be quite painful in many countries. In French Polynesia, for example, the duty was incredibly high, but if you were caught with undeclared alcohol, the fine was excruciating! We'd had no alcohol to declare at the time, so there was no problem. But this time we didn't know what the duty was, and we had plenty of rum.

TIGGER under sail, Fiji

Ultimately, Dave and I both believed honesty was the best policy, so we decided to declare the rum and hope that maybe the customs officials would just ignore it. It was, after all, just a few bottles, not cases and cases as some of the yachties, who had all simply lied, were carrying. (I'll take their names to my grave.) Of course, as it turned out they'd had the right idea, as we created quite a stir. Once we had put it on paper, the officials were forced to do something about it. And since normally nobody declares anything, they weren't sure what to do. Finally after much discussion in Fijian, they told us it would be $150 duty for the six bottles of rum we had on board, two being the maximum allowed duty-free. Dave asked if we could just pour it out, since it was only worth about 20 New Zealand dollars. But no, we couldn't do that, and the official then decided that he needed to inspect the boat. What a mess! Thank goodness we had declared all the rum, because if they had found more, it would have been even worse. The inspector was irritated that we had done something that caused him to act. We were outraged at the duty costs, and the other yachts thought we were nuts for declaring it in the first place. This was most definitely not the welcome we had hoped for in Fiji.

We anchored for a few days at Makongai Island, which has a clam farm, run by the government that is attempting to reintroduce giant tridacnas back to Fiji's reefs. The giant tridacnas are the ones of legend: a pearl diver, diving for a pearl for his beloved, accidentally put his foot in a tridacna, and it closed trapping him under water. I doubt if it could actually happen that way, but they are giants! The clam has a mantle, which spreads across the two halves of the shell, and in the middle is a valve through which water passes in and out, so the clam can collect food particles. The mantles are beautiful, all deep and velvety colors, with iridescent spots on them. They always closed slowly as we swished by them when snorkeling, and the

Farmers Market, Suva, Fiji

big ones didn't even close all the way. Once they did close, however, nothing could pry them apart.

One day, we dinghied over to the farm and asked for a tour. The fishery agents were very gracious; and we saw the tanks where the seed clams—about the size of a large grain of sand—start their life. In the next tank, they were larger, about the size of a cup. The next tank held even larger clams, and so forth. When the clams were about as big as a dinner plate, approximately 5 years old, they were planted onto selected reefs with the hopes that they would spawn the next generation, and the reefs would again sport these beautiful and important clams.

After that came more regatta fun at Musket Cove Resort on the island of Malolo Lailai on the west side of Fiji, before the run with the other yachts to Port Vila, on the island of Efate in Vanuatu. Dave and I were sitting in the cockpit one

Dave checking our way, Vanuatu

afternoon in the crowded anchorage at Musket Cove when I watched a dinghy wending its way through all the boats. One by one, heads popped up from down below to investigate the sound of an outboard going by. They looked like prairie dogs, popping up to sniff the air, then scurrying down below again. Our own prairie dog village in the middle of the South Pacific!

The exit from Musket Cove heading towards Vanuatu is a narrow winding path between reefs, nine miles long. To avoid the traffic jam, we were almost last in the line. As I looked forward at the boats, single file, in front of us, it looked like a wagon train winding across the plains, prairie schooners, with their sails up to catch the prairie winds.

Of course, only a few hours after that, all the sails had disappeared and we were once again alone on the sea.

While anchored off Port Vila in Vanuatu, friends on another yacht had $4,000 in cash stolen from their boat, and although it was eventually recovered when the thief tried to spend it, the police would not give it back, asking instead, "How can you prove it is your money?"

I liked some places better than others. After three weeks in Vanuatu, we pounded south into a headwind toward New Caledonia. The weather was not bad or dangerous, just rough, and we hove-to several times to get a little rest and on one occasion just to have a quiet dinner.

New Caledonia is a French protectorate that lies about 600 miles east of the northeast coast of Australia. Nouméa, its main city, is charming, sophisticated and friendly and the vast majority of New Caledonians live there. When we sailed to the Baie du Prony, at the south end of the main island, for a respite, we found the area almost completely uninhabited. There were, however, the ruins of an old prison, a sort of New Caledonian Devil's Island, which gave the area a distinct flavor all its own. In a nearby bay we jumped in the dinghy and rowed near the shore until we found a small river entrance that ran through the abandoned prison area. The stone buildings were tumbling down, and the jungle had overgrown most everything, but the hush in the air still held the message of suffering and despair. We rowed up the little river several times, and each time we came to the prison, we found ourselves whispering until we'd gone past. Only then did we feel free to laugh and talk out loud. Along the way we spotted several Venus flytrap plants, growing wild. They actually had insects trapped in their cup. It seemed a fitting plant to be growing around the old prison.

Our time with the boats from the cruising regatta, through Tonga, Fiji, Vanuatu, and New Caledonia, was the most social of our whole circumnavigation. There were about 45 yachts in the regatta, plus the ones that were traveling the route alone, so there were a lot of us out there. We'd had potlucks on the

Baie du Prony, New Caledonia

beach in the Ha'apai Group of Tonga, pizza parties at anchor in the Vava'u Group, sundowners in Fiji, and morning tea in New Caledonia. There were New Zealanders, Australians, Canadians, Americans and a couple of European yachts.

It seemed every anchorage we sailed into had some friends already anchored. We couldn't get away from each other! It was hard in a way, since I often need solitude. And there were times when I was disappointed when we entered an anchorage only to find other people already there. Still I liked all these people, and though Dave and I would say to each other, "Let's not run around again," we would soon be at someone's yacht or they would be at ours.

Toward the end of it though, I was definitely feeling the effects of over-exposure, all the more so because my friend Joanna was still sailing the waters around Tonga, and I didn't have anyone to complain to anymore!

I think I had also lost my obsession for the South Pacific. When I reached the Marquesas, I would never have imagined those words leaving my lips. But the pull of moving west was once again strong. I had been gone three years from the United States and all that was dear and familiar to me, and my goal was to sail around the world, not to find a spot to settle down in, even for a short while. When I was happy, I was still enchanted with the islands, but when one more dugout came to the boat to sell something or ask for something, I was losing my enthusiasm. Call me a spoil sport, but that cruising season was not my favorite and I got stomach pains, headaches and dizzy spells. I was making it hard for Dave too by the time we got to New Caledonia. For some strange reason, he put up with it and didn't send me packing. The main thing was that we were moving west. Maybe the next ocean would be better.

20

Heading for the Land of Oz

It was late October when we finally left the huge lagoon protecting Nouméa to sail on a brisk southeast wind. The 820 miles to Brisbane were another record run for TIGGER—five days from anchor-up in New Caledonia to dock lines secured at the customs dock in Australia. The first 24 hours were a dream sail, steady 10- to 15-knot breezes with flat seas and no rolling. I wrote in my journal that "a night like this is what sailing is all about, these pristine moments that hopefully last for days."

Unfortunately, in this particular case it was hours, not days, for right after I wrote those lines, the wind picked up and seas got rough, and we sailed the rest of the way with a reefed jib and storm trysail. We didn't touch the sails for three days, and even though we discussed putting up the storm staysail, neither one of us wanted to go forward on the rolling deck with water flying everywhere. Safety first, comfort second, speed third. Besides, even with the small sail area, we were making good time.

We again had a perfect sail the last 80 miles before we spotted the Coulundra Light; the winds calmed and the seas flattened again. We breathed a sigh, first of relief and then of contentment as we scoured the horizon for land.

The continental shelf extends far out to sea beyond Australia's east coast, and we were on soundings long before we spotted land. When we did, we raised the Australian courtesy flag to the strains of our version of *Waltzing Matilda* and mentally prepared ourselves for civilization again.

Coming even closer there was a large fleet of shrimpers working the waters both in Moreton Bay, the entrance to Brisbane, and close offshore. So, in the late evening darkness, we dodged these boats, brightly lit and looking like fireflies, flitting back and forth across our path. Finally, we entered the shipping channel that would take us 42 miles across the bay and up the river to the customs dock. Between the shrimpers and the quickly shoaling waters, we kept busy. But at midnight I went to nap while Dave navigated up the channel.

At 5 a.m. I was up and looking through the binoculars at the Glasshouse Mountains in the west. These mountains contain lots of mica and the sun lit them up like a spotlight on crystal. So this was Australia!

Customs and quarantine were reportedly as thorough in Australia as in New Zealand, so we had the lockers cleaned out before pulling up to the dock, where they gave us a polite and friendly welcome while inspecting the lockers and pulling up cushions for any hidden spots. I assured them I had no canned goods that contained bacon but the quarantine officer still did a thorough inspection, shining a flashlight in the back of lockers. As soon as he left, I opened the closest cupboard and there, right in front, was a can of bean with bacon soup! How did I miss that? How did he miss it? We ate the evidence for lunch.

We were in Australia for eight months, and I had a chance to fall in love with this feisty country with its narrow coastal band of sophisticated living and vast outback. Both faces of Australia were fun and fascinating to me. We wanted to do a lot of sightseeing, but as usual, finances dictated how far and in what style we wandered.

Neither Dave nor I were keen to drive in this country of left-sided traffic. So we decided, as we had in New Zealand, not to rent a car, but to try to get around on the train and bus systems. Our marina was 40 miles from Brisbane in a little town called Manly. We would walk about a mile, catch the commuter train into Brisbane and do our shopping or just walk around.

Brisbane is a beautiful, bustling city, on the southern edge of the more tropical part of Australia. In the winter, the locals said it got quite cold, but it was a very hot summer, and several times we set out for Brisbane, only to turn around and come back because it was too darn hot.

I really needed to go home for the holidays that year, since we hadn't gone home from New Zealand and my homesickness had put a damper on the previous season. As a result we left TIGGER in good hands at the East Coast Marina and took a taxi to the airport to catch a flight back to the United States. The taxi driver wore an orange bowling shirt, black pegged pants and an Elvis hair cut. He was my age, and ready to rock and

A new friend, Koala Reserve, Brisbane, Australia

roll! Like taxi drivers everywhere he was also ready to talk. He told us he belonged to a rock and roll dance group that performed all over Australia. We had a great time reminiscing about Elvis, Buddy Holly, the Everly Brothers, the Big Bopper and all the other greats. Since Dave is a classical music snob, the conversation flowed between just the driver and me. I had a musical trip down memory lane on the way to the airport, and felt quite young for a few miles.

Upon our return in January, the plan was to see Sydney, then Tasmania, and then my long time dream, Ayers Rock, in the center of Australia. After a lengthy session with the travel agent, and counting up the cost of all this, we finally had to leave Tasmania for another time.

We played tourist in Sydney and saw the Opera House and the Botanical Gardens, and learned a little more about the history of the settling of the country. Australia's past is laden with violence and hardship. It was first used by the British as a penal colony; a handy solution to their crime problem in the 1800s. Whether they were vicious murderers or unfortunate debtors, off the convicts went to Australia and somehow, some survived and carved out a new country.

Of course, to the Aborigines, it was not a new country. After all, they had been there for at least 10,000 years. Sadly for them, it has not been a country in which either side has shown much tolerance toward the other, although I tried not to judge either side, because the United States has a lot to answer for also. Today is today, and one person being good to one other person is the only way to save the world, as far as I am concerned.

Leaving TIGGER in the marina in Manly we saw Sydney and then Ayers Rock, taking a flight and then a car to the Uluru National Park, about 2,000 miles of outback from the coast.

When I was 12 years old, I saw a picture of "the world's largest monolith," in a *National Geographic* Magazine. And since that day, Ayers Rock has been on my dream list of places to visit. I feel so lucky when I can fulfill a long-held dream. It's a fascinating rock, glowing red in the noontime sun and changing in a hot, theatrical show of earth colors as the sun moves across the sky. Red, cinnamon, rust, maroon, purple: All day long, it appears lit from within, shimmering and glowing until the setting sun gently turns out the lights.

The Aborigines originally named it Uluru, and it is a sacred place to them. We had first intended to climb the rock as its size and shape just begs to be climbed. But the Aborigines ask that you not climb it, as they feel responsible for whoever is on the rock. It says something about their gentleness and courtesy to strangers, that there are no obtrusive "No Climbing" signs, even though thousands of people ignore the Aborigines wishes. There are plenty of places around the center where the message is posted, though. So the people who do climb know they are acting against the wishes of the Aborigines. Watching this unique natural formation in its sunrise glory, or in the drama of sunset, we both felt the mystical presence of the ancients and were content to just gaze and appreciate.

However, everything has its price, and it being February and the middle of the Australian summer, we had about 110 degrees each day—true desert conditions. And the flies! Wow, the flies! I'd heard it said the fly is the national bird of Australia, and now I believe it. And they are of the small, sticky kind that can drive one to madness. They loved our faces, and we spent most of the time outside swishing them away. We bought nets, like beekeeper nets, to put over our heads, and laughed wildly each time we looked at each other. Now the flies gathered on the net and you only had to swish about half as much. Sometimes we would think the other tourists were waving to us, but they were just swishing flies. My remembrance of the rock is comprised of three basic elements: beauty, heat and flies. It seemed to me that nothing in Australia was common or ordinary.

21

The Great, Great Barrier Reef

By March, it was time to start moving up the coast. We had about 1,200 miles to go, anchoring almost every night, and we needed to be in Darwin by June or July at the latest, in order to make the Indian Ocean crossing and be in South Africa by November—away from the cyclone season near the equator.

That at least was the plan. It had taken us three and a half years to go halfway around the world, and now I wanted to do the second half in a year. Dave was willing, so we decided to forgo Indonesia and head that season across the Indian Ocean for Durban, South Africa, and then around the Cape of Good Hope, and across the South Atlantic Ocean. Gad, we were practically home!

First, however, we had to get around to the other side of Australia. And while I knew it was a big country, looking at the 62 charts we needed just to sail around one third of the coast gave "big" a whole new meaning. This was the biggest landmass we had encountered since North America. At least we had the Whitsunday Islands and the Great Barrier Reef to look forward to, as well as the knowledge that some of the best sailing was still to come.

Both of us reread Captain Cook's account of his discovery of Australia and his first journey up the coast where he got trapped behind the Great Barrier Reef. It was exciting and scary, and a miracle that he made it out; no charts, not sure what was ahead, only his courage and his crew's faith in him. We had charts galore, GPS and a coastal path already laid out for us with red and green markers, a nice improvement over the last 300 years.

The weather had already started to turn when we left Brisbane in early April, and until we got behind the Great Barrier Reef a month later, we made frequent stops, sometimes several days at a time, to wait out blustery early autumn conditions. Each morning, we would chart a course that would take us north to another anchorage, dig in by dark and sleep well before venturing out the next day if the weather allowed.

Soon we were in the Sandy Straits, between Fraser Island and the mainland, a route that saved some miles but was a mess of sand bars and tidal currents. Our second day in the straits, working our way toward an anchorage, we went aground on a sand bar. The tide was going out, so we sat there, heeling more and more as the tide receded. Finally, the water came up and little by little we straightened up until we were floating free again. Easy stuff, just sand, and this time we didn't try to power off and end up with more silt in the seawater pump. That night we sheltered in a little anchorage in the mangroves, but didn't go ashore because there were loads of mosquitoes and nothing much to see on shore besides a lot of trees.

The next morning we moved farther north to anchor off a lovely holiday spot called Kingfisher Resort. I was starting to get a scratchy throat and feared I had the flu. All I wanted was a place to anchor where I could spend the next 10 days feeling sorry for myself, while the flu did its thing. As we were circling the anchorage, I glanced under the dodger where I had left a pair of shoes and saw something moving. Oh my God, it was a snake! I let out a shriek that brought Dave running from the bow where he had been getting ready to drop anchor. I pointed "There's a snake in my shoe! Do something, kill it, do something, do something!" I was practically dancing in fright, whereas Dave was looking at it in that peculiar male way that denotes interest but not fear. What is it with men and reptiles? I have been terrified of snakes ever since my dear sister threw a garden snake at me when I was 3, and it wrapped itself around my neck. I have a hard time even looking at them in books.

Dave was still trying to figure out what kind of snake it was and said, "What do you want me to do?" So I shrieked again, in case he hadn't quite understood my earlier orders, "Do something, kill it, *kill it.* " Dave took the unoccupied shoe and hit the snake on the head with it. The poor little guy looked stunned for a moment, and Dave took that opportunity to empty the snake-filled shoe over the side, and the last we saw of him, he was groggily swimming away. I am sure he got into our dinghy at the mangrove-lined anchorage and then, while we weren't looking, climbed up the dinghy painter to make himself at home on our deck and in my shoe.

With that crisis over (remember, Australia has loads of poisonous things and that could have been one of them), we anchored and I collapsed on the settee to let the virus take its toll. I only had enough strength to order Dave around in a weak voice and accept the delicious meals he prepared for his "honey." It took almost three weeks before I felt strong enough for us to leave and continue heading through the straits back to open water.

Things were looking up in the seasick department for me. I was hardly ever seasick day-tripping up the coast. I didn't know it then, but my mal de mer was to plague me less and less, as I became an old salt at last.

From the end of April until the middle of May of that year, the comet Hale-Bopp was giving a spectacular show in the southern sky, and we were in the perfect spot. In secluded anchorages away from city lights, the comet was our after-dinner treat. We would try to anchor by 4 p.m., get a few things done and have dinner finished by 6:30. Then we could sit in the cockpit, each with binoculars, and gaze at this heavenly spectacle. How incredible and beautiful it was, a silver streak in the twilight. I know it is all explainable—it is just science, after all—but it was more than that to me. I felt an intimacy with the heavens, as if somehow I was absorbing some part of this magical thing. When we could no longer see it, I felt a grief like a dear friend had left me, and I was lonely in the evenings for quite a while.

Each little harbor or anchorage had its own charm. Small fishing villages, windswept anchorages behind sand dunes; Australia has hundreds of places to anchor along the coast going north from Brisbane. In the little fishing village of Bowen, we had to drag our way through mud to reach the dock (they said it had six feet at low tide), but once we tied up, the folks were friendly. They let us have water and spend the night where we were instead of dropping the hook at the anchorage. As we walked through the dusty streets, on a quiet Sunday afternoon, I saw the kookaburra birds watching us and heard them "laughing." I remembered a line from a childhood song: "kookaburras laughing in the old gum tree." I didn't realize a bird could make that sound of human laughter.

We had forgotten about docks and the rats of Takaroa, and we had more visitors in the night. I didn't hear them, but we found their droppings the next day. Fortunately none stayed aboard, although we did keep our big, mean-looking rat trap under the sink. It wasn't set, but we were ready if any decided to stay.

Dave gets up very early (crack of dawn early), while I like to sleep a little later. He has the adorable habit of kissing my hair (my face is buried in a pillow) before he goes to the galley to make his morning tea. One morning, I dreamed that the rat was still onboard and when he kissed my hair, I threw my arms up to fling that rat away from me. Dave yelped as I hit him, and that woke me. I mumbled, "I thought you were a rat." He claims that was the first time he had ever been described by that term, but considering his age and probable experiences, I have my doubts.

In Gladstone, we helped the city observe Anzac Day. We went with an Aussie friend and then joined in the parade as the whole crowd marched to the town park. There were hundreds of people in the parade, both marchers and spectators, old men in long white beards and young children skipping alongside Grandpa. At the park, veterans of long-ago wars gave speeches, bagpipers played mournful music, and we were quite moved by the respect and reverence given to this day by everyone, old and young. *Waltzing Matilda* is the national song, and as such it was played much more slowly than the rousing version I have always heard. Now it was sung with love. I couldn't keep the tears from my eyes.

In Gladstone, we finally threw away one of the two autopilots on board after it burned up a control board. Enough was enough. Now we only had one questionable autopilot so there would be no more cannibalizing for parts.

I will try to be fair about the autopilot. When we bought it, the model was listed as the correct one for TIGGER's size. But several years later, the manufacturer no longer recommended the in-the-cockpit style for a 37-foot yacht; rather, the company recommended the below-decks model. So although we had bought ours in good faith, it probably was always too light for our yacht. Still, our trouble was not that it didn't steer well, but that its components kept breaking. Once, on a long passage, we had to replace a pin that had completely rusted through and crumbled in Dave's hand. It was not even stainless, for God's sake! Dave used a stainless steel sail-repair needle to repair it and the pin lasted until we stopped using the unit. Come to think of it, I won't defend it.

Dave called me to the cockpit one evening at dusk. Stretched across the sky was a huge dark cloud. However, it wasn't a rain cloud. Looking through the binoculars I could see that it was a great fleet of bats, the large flying foxes. There must have been half a million of them! It took a full 30 minutes for them to clear the sky near our boat as they headed for the off-shore islands to forage for food. Each night about the same time, they would leave their caves and head toward the sea, and we would watch this giant cloud, black against the crimson and salmon twilight sky. Bats are beautiful—from a distance!

The towns were nice stops, with marinas for showers and laundry and fresh provisions. But I was always happy to head back out to quiet anchorages. As soon as we got behind the Great Barrier Reef, we had the best sailing imaginable. Each day was golden with sun, southeast winds of 20 to 25 knots and flat seas. All we had to do was set the main and jib, sit back and rip along at 7 knots. But we needed to be careful. Those buoy markers were guiding us around reefs. I would revel in the glorious days, in a state of low-level ecstasy, sometimes shutting my eyes for just a moment, and letting this perfection settle over me. At the end of the day, a sandy patch near a small windswept island awaited us, where we would be safe for the night.

At one anchorage, we met up with Paul and Susan on ELENOA. Paul is a clever man, who always had some nifty item that he had made himself, and which would make me turn to Dave and say, "Hey, why don't you make one of those?" I copied their pattern for beanbag chairs, sewing them from what was left of our recently replaced mainsail cover, and I've loved them ever since. Susan made her own granola, grew herbs and generally put me to shame in the self-sufficiency department. The couple had kept one secret item, though, something they had bought, a 12-volt ice cream maker! Since there were only two other yachts in the anchorage, Kay and Jerry on ROMANCE, and TIGGER, it was the right time to pop the surprise. Over we all went to their boat for afternoon tea featuring fresh homemade chocolate ice cream, a treat I shall never forget.

Another dream-list item was fulfilled when we stopped at Lizard Island, about 50 miles off the coast, near the outer reef.

This is the island Captain Cook climbed to find his way through the reef and out of the maze he had been trapped in. The resort on the island is an exclusive diving resort, and yachties are asked not to enter the grounds. After all, people from around the world pay $600 to $700 a day to stay there, so I guess they want it to themselves. Still, Dave decided to go over and ask if we could get on one of their dive boats so I could live my dream of diving on the Great Barrier Reef. I had been an avid scuba diver in my younger years, diving all through Micronesia, and in the Mediterranean. I had given it up when the responsibilities of being a single mom with a demanding career pulled me away. But I could still snorkel. And it was the Great Barrier Reef. They surprised us by saying yes.

A few of the other yachts had sailed to the outer reef themselves to do their diving and snorkeling, and we had just about talked ourselves into doing that too, but one of the yachts got grounded on a reef with the tide going out and darkness coming on. We listened on the VHF radio as a passing Australian warship pulled them off. It was a steel yacht, so they did not get holed, but it wiped all thoughts of risking TIGGER right out of our minds.

Anchorage, Lizard Island behind the Great Barrier Reef, Australia

What a wild ride out to the reef, in the resort's 35-foot dive boat, heading into southeast winds of about 25 knots. Riding on a powerboat is so different than being on a sailboat. No tacking for powerboats, just plow right into it all! One of the women from the resort was so seasick that she spent the entire trip laying flat on a settee below, hugging a bucket. I didn't know anyone could actually be that green.

Once we were in the water everything was spectacular. The reef was everything I dreamed it would be. We swam with giant potato cod, huge fish that were 300 to 400 pounds, silver with black polka dots. The dive master led the scuba divers down to the sandy sea bottom, where he took some bait out of his bag, and 20 giant potato cod gathered round, while he passed out fish snacks. Then the fish cruised through the group and swam to the surface, so close we could touch them. There were also hump-headed parrot fish, weighing in at about 100 pounds each. Many of the fish we had seen in spots throughout the Pacific, but every species was so much bigger.

The climax of the day came when we got back and anchored in the resort's lagoon. The dive master gathered us on the dive platform, and for some reason yelled at me as I swished my sandals in the water to rinse them. That was odd, I thought, until he swished a fish carcass in the water and an 800-pound grouper came roaring up from the bottom, leapt out of the water with gaping mouth and gulped the morsel down as he splashed back in, drenching all of us screaming observers.

After that came Cape York, which was another thrill. When we anchored in the lee of the cape in front of the Pajinka Wilderness Lodge, I felt like we had really done something special. We stayed there for 10 days, some days going ashore to visit the lodge or climb to the "top of Australia," a cliff top where a marker points the way to Hong Kong, San Francisco and other far away places. One day we caught a ride into the Aboriginal village of Bamaga. Dusty and depressed, the village was mainly supported by the Australian government; it had no jobs or commerce. Some days we just hung out on TIGGER, watching the wind blow. It does that a lot up there in early June.

We had made arrangements to join another rally to go "over the top," as they call the route across the northern coast of Australia, which meant we had to be in Gove by June 20, so our time was scheduled again. There was also the Gulf of Carpenteria to cross, a pretty rough body of water, according to the Aussies. After our 10 days at Cape York, we took off for Gove on the western side of the Gulf of Carpenteria.

Leaving behind the calm waters inside the Great Barrier Reef, we were once again out in the turbulent ocean, and it was rock and roll the whole 367 miles. The winds were up and down, but the rough seas didn't vary, so we just endured. I wasn't spared the mal de mer this time. The second day was squally, with rain pelting us and just plain miserable conditions. On the third day, the sun came out and the last miles were better except for the tension of dodging reefs and finding our way into the Gove anchorage.

Gove is a company town, built to support the local bauxite mine, so in spite of its isolation it still had excellent markets, a hospital and good schools; no chandleries, but good provisioning.

"Over the top" rally, north coast of Australia

We joined the 30 other boats on June 29 to cross the start line of the rally and sail 23 miles to the first anchorage. The route took us through the Hole in the Wall, a shortcut be-tween two islands, saving 50 or 60 miles. It had to be transited when the tide was just right, and even then you only had about an hour to pass through the mile-long channel. Of course, there were 30 other yachts that had to pass through within this hour; so the experience was not for the faint of heart, which is just what I became when I saw the entrance waves, the narrow channel, and the other yachts, all converging on this one spot. The seas were running fairly high when we entered. TIGGER was one of the last to enter since we were trying to avoid the crush, but once in the channel all was calm, with a light breeze, and all we had to do was squeeze ourselves through with the others. Still for a Texas gal who likes wide-open spaces, this was too tight for me.

On July 4, we stopped at the anchorage at South Gulborn Island, and it was a big celebration day for everyone: Ameri-can Independence Day, Canadian Day and Australian North-ern Territory Self Rule Day. The Americans organized a traditional Fourth of July picnic with patriotic music and out-of-date flares to shoot off for fireworks. We planted American flags on the beach, and the rest of the group took it all in stride.

Close to the end of the rally, we stopped at an anchorage for a barbecue and talent show. I don't remember the name of the anchorage, but the image will be with me forever. The beach was narrow, backed up by high cliffs, and it was evening when we took the dinghy over to where the bonfire was built. The night was very dark, no moon. Our little outboard stirred up the phosphorescence, and once again, the trail of silver-green lingered behind for a long time. I watched the glow be-hind us and then turned and looked toward the fire. The performers for the talent show stood between the fire and the cliff behind them. The shadows they cast against the cliffs were huge and ghostly. The night was black all around and the fire was the only light. The people gathered close and the whole scene looked primitive and ancient. The star-studded sky, the dark water, sparkled by phosphorescence, the shadows on the cliff, and the distant sound of laughter—we were small and lonely outside the "circle" and we were drawn in.

The top of Australia is mostly desolate, sparsely inhabited. It is all Aboriginal Reserve and incredibly beautiful. We anchored almost every night of the 12-day rally, had barbecues, told stories, met some of the Aborigines who live up there and ended up in Darwin, the last stop in Australia.

22

⚘

Braving the Indian Ocean

Darwin, on the northwest corner of Australia, is a jumping-off spot for sailors leaving Australia. In July, there were three different groups: the 100 or so yachts participating in the Darwin-Ambon Race, with a first prize of 10,000 Australian dollars; cruisers who have permits for Indonesia; and sailors who plan to bypass Indonesia, and head straight out into the Indian Ocean. We, of course, were in the third group that planned to sail either southwest to round the Cape of Good Hope or west and north to the Red Sea to transit the Suez Canal. Most of our friends were heading for Indonesia, so there were many goodbye parties and promises to stay in touch, as well as a whole new group to meet and travel with; mostly Europeans— British, Swiss, German, Austrian and Swedish—along with several South Africans returning home after their circumnavigations.

In all the books and articles I had read about cruising, I never really got the picture of just how many of us are out there, not just Americans, but other nationalities as well. It seems more and more of the world's sailors have the resources and the desire to go offshore. Of course, improved communications have also played a part. In fact, even while we were out sailing, technology continued to improve by big leaps as e-mail for offshore sailors became a possibility. We hemmed and hawed and finally bought the extra equipment we needed to send e-mail via radio. I had gotten my Ham general level license the day before leaving the United States so the network was available to us.

I was of two minds about having such instant communications with people back home. On one hand, I was afraid it would take away from some of the things I loved about being offshore. On the other hand, I was still struggling with homesickness and thought it might help. In the end it did both those things. Using our radio and our computer, we would send out a message to an amateur radio operator in Perth, Australia, who forwarded it on to another in South Africa. This operator would then transfer it to the Internet where our message could be read by friends and family. They in turn sent their e-mail messages to an address in South Africa where it was forwarded to Perth, then I could pick it up using the computer and radio. It was all fairly easy, and my excessive homesickness pretty much disappeared, although it meant installing more stuff, and making sure it worked before we left Darwin.

One windless day in early August, we set out for South Africa, across the wide Indian Ocean. Our first stop was to be Christmas Island, 1,500 miles due west. We would pass south of the Indonesian islands of Bali and Timor, and cross the Sahul Banks, which lay 350 miles or so west of Darwin.

We motored out of Darwin, but soon found the southeast winds, so up went a full main and jib and in no time we were moving along happily at 6 knots. There was a fair west setting current to help us along, and I didn't feel seasick—so far, so good.

After that optimistic start, however, the wind died, the current petered out and we made poor distances for the next few days. In fact, the third day out we only made 56 miles. But, that was okay. It was so beautiful out there.

Early on, we came across a fleet of Australian warships on maneuvers. I called on the radio to ask if we should take a course around them. A voice from the lead ship replied, "No problem, just come on the same course," even though it was right through the middle of the fleet. "Okay," I answered doubtfully, and kept on our course. Ten minutes later I looked to the south and saw a puff of smoke from one of the ship's guns! Seconds later a great boom followed. Good God, they were shooting at us! No wonder they wanted us to stay on this course. We were their target! Another ship farther to the south let go a volley and there was another puff of smoke and a boom. This time, however, I could tell that both guns were pointed away from us toward some target I couldn't see. Still, I was quite happy when we lost them on our eastern horizon. "Soon we will be all alone again," I said to Dave, "and have lots of sea room. That's where I need to be."

The southeast winds did settle in on the fourth day and began moving us steadily toward Christmas Island. We only had the Sahul Banks in our way and then deep water and no worries. The days blended together, one sunny day after another. The seas were gentle, even though we had the good trades now. I wanted to sail like this all the way to South Africa. I read, Dave puttered and nothing broke. We could also, finally, shed our clothes again. Life was good.

Still we were not as alone out there as I'd thought we'd be, and several fishing boats passed by with an intense curiosity toward us. By the way they had decorated their boats, they were probably Indonesian, although they flew no flags. We would see them come over the horizon on a heading that would take them far to the north or south of us. Then suddenly they would make a dramatic turn and head straight in our direction. Damn! They were probably just curious fishermen, but we were near Indonesia, and pirates were known to lurk these waters, and well. . . . The drill never changed: duck down, get our flares and grab the binoculars. Then we would slouch in the cockpit so they couldn't see there were only two of us. Inevitably they would come much closer to us than we liked and we would change course a bit to see what they would do. But then they would just take a look, never wave or acknowledge that we were there, and go on their way. Back on course we would head, breathing a sigh of relief.

When we passed south of Timor, we had another jolting experience, although the danger was not ours, but someone else's. On that particular afternoon, we were having dinner in the cockpit in preparation for Dave to start his off-watch evening sleep. Suddenly, Dave pointed to a spot over my shoulder and said, "What the heck is that?" I turned and there, off our port side about half a mile, was a raft, palm frond for a sail, and sitting on the sides were people!

With all the unrest on Timor at that time, our first thought was "boat people."

"Dave," I cried. "We have to go over there and see what's going on."

"But they're heading toward Australia," he replied.

"It doesn't matter, turn around, we have to go to them, what if they are out of water, or sick or lost? Who in their right mind would set sail in that?"

Quickly we rolled up the jib, started the engine and turned around to chase the raft, as it was now well past us. Dusk was upon us, and it was a race to try to catch them before the darkness closed in completely.

"Hurry, Dave, we have to get to them before we lose them in the darkness." With the engine revved up, soon we were gaining on them, all the time discussing what we would do with 15 or so boat people. Would we have enough blankets? Where could we put them? Did we have enough water? Was anyone sick? What about children? Oh, we knew we could do it, but they would have to sail to Christmas Island. There was no way we could sail upwind all the way back to Australia.

As we got closer, Dave said, "I don't think those are people, or something's very wrong, they aren't moving." But peering through the binoculars into the twilight, I was sure I could see the figures, sitting tall around the raft. Just then one waved to me, and I triumphantly replied, "Look, look, didn't you see that one just wave? They need us!"

We finally caught up with the raft, and sure enough, you guessed it, the 15 or so cormorants that had been hitching a free ride on this handy flotsam, flew away. The waving figure had been a bird flapping his wings. Perspective is lost at sea without any object to relate to other than the sea and sky. At twilight, a small raft close up with 15 cormorants looked just like a large raft with 15 people, far away.

After a minute of hysterical laughter, we took a closer look at the raft, and I got the camera out to take some pictures. I'm almost always too late with the camera, but this time, I was ready. I was now convinced that the raft had been manned, perhaps someone setting a rafting record, and that the sailor had been lost overboard.

Among other things it was well constructed of bamboo logs and was about 15 feet long and 6 feet wide. The sail was a palm frond lashed to a pole at the front end. There was another frond trailing on a short line aft, acting as a drogue. On the middle of the raft was a deck box with the name "Alex Poe, Jr." painted on the side and "5021MEFI" on the top. There was also "5021" on the mast and "Golden Lizard" painted on the side of the logs. Whoever this raft belonged to, it seemed he wanted to be identified from the air.

Soon we were getting ahead of the raft, so I told Dave, "Stay close, it's getting dark and I want to take more pictures." Moments later the raft was coming up behind us and we couldn't get out of the way. Bam! It hit our wind steering unit, knocking the servo-oar askew. Later, when Dave loosened the nut to put it right, he dropped his best wrench into the deep blue. Finally, we got everything sorted out, and the raft disappeared into the night as we continued sailing west.

The next morning, I reported the sighting to Robbie's Net, a cruiser's net on the 14 Mhz band out of Mooloolaba, Australia. I did so for two reasons. First, if the raft really had been manned at one time, then someone needed to know about it, and soon. Also, if that heavy raft hit a yacht, it would do serious damage, so other cruisers needed to be on the lookout. The speculation on the net was that it was a fishing raft, detached from an oil rig off Indonesia. We saw two more the next day, but no hitchhikers.

I was gloating that at least I got pictures of this strange craft, until I checked the camera. Of course, there was no film in it. Rats!

About 200 miles out of Christmas Island, we had squalls with heavy rain and winds up to 30 knots. My log recorded a 190-mile day, a record at that time. Sailing into Christmas Island, however, we had a light breeze and overcast skies, 12 days to the hour from Darwin.

By this time Dave was admitting he'd made a big mistake when we left Darwin. We'd left with more electronic stuff than ever before but had failed to replace our 2-year-old battery with a new one. By the time we got to Christmas Island, he was really wishing he'd done so. Our four days in the small rolly anchorage were spent trying to track down a marine grade battery. No luck, though the islanders that we met, mostly Australians, were very helpful and kind.

They had eight moorings in the anchorage for visiting yachts but the morning we arrived they were all taken, mostly by local fishing boats. The anchorage is deep and strewn with coral and coral rubble, so it was a job to find a patch of sand. We thought we did, in 45 feet of water. But that night, the chain started grinding on both the coral and our nerves. After three more days of this it was time to go.

When Dave went to pay the harbormaster the man said, "That will be $50 for the week's mooring."

"But we didn't have a mooring," Dave protested. "We had to anchor because the moorings are mostly taken up by local fishing boats. And we have only been here four days."

The harbormaster calmly replied, "You still have to pay for a mooring and for a week."

Of course, Mr. Consumer Advocate Ragle took exception, paying $50, but promptly marching over to the island commissioner to lodge a complaint. The $50 was not at issue. The charges for services we didn't receive was. The Commissioner was polite, took lots of notes and told Dave he would look into it. We left the island, and I'm sure life went on as usual.

23

❧

Let the Winds Blow

If the sail to Christmas Island had been the yin, then the 450-mile sail to Cocos-Keeling was surely the yang. As soon as we left all hell broke loose, with big seas and 30-knot winds. The first night out, I was seasick and miserable, but at least the sky cleared so I could see the stars. The next day the squalls started again, and we had copious rains, high winds and rough seas. In the middle of it all, the boom bail, which holds both the mainsheet and preventer blocks in place, gave way with a loud bang, and the boom flew to its extreme against the shroud. The full mainsail was up, the wind was driving it against the spreader and the shroud, and we had to figure out a way to get it down before it did any serious damage. Dave was at the mast while I tried to drive the boat into the wind using the engine while the seas kept throwing TIGGER back. It was all quite horrible, what with the rolling, my worrying about Dave and the driving rain. We both had on only our underwear under our harnesses, and we were soaking wet and cold. Dave finally got the sail down and the boom secured. Then we put up the trysail so we could get underway again. In all it took about two hours, and still we had lines all over the deck that needed to be sorted and cleared, while the rain kept coming down. Afterward we dried off, put on warm clothes and drank cup after cup of hot tea. But it still took many hours before I was really warm again.

Some time during this storm, a red-footed booby hitched a ride on the stern rail, and even when Dave was only two feet away, he would just sit there and preen. He flew away about six hours later, leaving numerous "gifts" on the railing and the man-overboard packet we had stowed there. He came back later, sat on the boom and stayed another six hours. I told Dave he was going to have to clean up after the bird this time, since he was the one who hated to shoo him away, being the bird lover that he is. When I wasn't looking, Mr. Booby hopped onto the solar panels above my head and emitted several loud squawks. I about jumped out of my cold and wet skin!

We sailed the rest of the way with the trysail only, and when we approached Cocos-Keeling in a squall, we entered the narrow channel anyway, so sick were we of the weather. My nerves remained intact until we went from off-soundings to 22 feet of water in less than a quarter mile. Boy, I hate that! I need time to get used to the idea of shallow water. We trusted the GPS and charts, however, and safely anchored in front of Direction Island, just inside the atoll.

There were a total of 22 boats in the anchorage, most, like us, going to South Africa, although several were headed for the Maldives or the Seychelles. We found a deep-cycle battery on Home Island, where the Malays live. And we provisioned at West Island, where the Australians are. Cocos-Keeling is a typical atoll, with one good navigable entrance, and several islands and islets strewn in a circle around a big lagoon.

The only place in the atoll where yachts were allowed to anchor was right in front of Direction Island. But that was fine, because it was the prettiest island in the whole ocean as far as I was concerned. Uninhabited and part of an old copra plantation, it was covered with coconut palms. The water was turquoise and the beach pure white sand. Coral heads in the shallow water near shore provided homes for damselfish, clown fish, puffer fish and others to watch and laugh at while snorkeling. Damselfish are very protective of their little piece of coral. Even though they are only an inch long, if you get too close they will dart out at you looking quite ferocious.

Someone had built a small, thatched shelter among the palms, with a picnic table and a few chairs for lounging while gazing at the lagoon. For the past 20 years or so, yachts had left their calling cards in the form of flotsam with their names and the year they stopped by. We hung ours from the rafter, a co-conut shell—TIGGER, Dave and Sharon, 1997. We were next to the ice skates that Tristan Jones had left in some bygone year. One strange note to the setting was a solar-powered phone booth in the middle of this deserted island. That begged for a phone call back to the children. So we did.

By this time Dave had made a temporary fix to the broken boom bail by wrapping a line around the boom, to which we attached the mainsheet and preventer blocks. The line was thick and strong, and we checked it periodically for chafe until we could do a permanent fix in South Africa.

It was early September, and the winds blew hard the entire two weeks we were there. Several times, it was 40 knots in the

Dave hanging our flotsam, marking our passage, Cocos-Keeling

Solar-powered telephone, Direction Island, Cocos-Keeling

anchorage. "Darn," I thought, "if we only had a wind generator, we would have power to spare. We could run the watermaker and not have to make a rough, wet trip to Home Island
for water before the very long passage to Mauritius." With our
battery bank still less than optimal, even with the new battery,
I was coveting a wind generator more and more. South Africa
was going to provide us with one, I just knew it. In the meantime, however, we took the Saturday ferry over to Home Island, five miles away. That was the only day it came to
Direction Island. There we filled the water jugs, hauled them
back on the ferry to our anchorage, then dumped them in the
dinghy and rowed back to TIGGER.

We rowed because the outboard was giving us fits again.
It was relatively new, having been purchased to replace the
old one while we were in New Zealand. With the wind always
brisk in the anchorage, it was a real chore to row upwind to
TIGGER, but we never knew when the temperamental outboard would work and when it wouldn't. Finally in Mauritius,
a friend suggested a trick to starting it, and that solved the
problem. Being an engineer, Dave was uncomfortable with

Prisoner Island, Cocos-Keeling

this solution since he didn't fully understand it, maintaining, "It isn't supposed to do that." But I am mostly a realist and said, "It does, so use the tricky way of starting it." Dave spent hours trying to track down the problem and solve it the proper way, but to this day, we continue to use the trick. What can I say?

The trick is really very simple. We fully choke the outboard and then pull the starter cord once. (It never starts the first time.) Then we close the choke and pull the starter cord again. Zip! It starts right up. Before, Dave would always leave the choke open until it started, which sometimes worked and sometimes didn't. With this new method, it starts every time. But this revelation had to wait until Mauritius.

Cocos-Keeling is very high on my list of favorite places. I loved the isolation (even with the other yachts in the anchorage), the uninhabited island, the wild wind and the high surf on the seaward side of the island. Inside the lagoon the water was mostly calm, and I would come back from a stroll on the beach, windblown, wet and sunburned. Down below on TIGGER was my haven; neat and quiet, brass lights shining on the teak bulkheads, and Dave and I in harmony. This was our sanctuary, our little nest. I always feel so safe on TIGGER. I love that feeling.

Mauritius was the next planned stop on our passage to South Africa. We left Cocos-Keeling on a windy early September day, and we had mostly good trades as we sailed south and west. It was 2,300 miles to Mauritius, which we figured would be about 20 days of sailing. Eight other yachts left within a day of our departure, since we were all feeling the need to keep moving in order to be in Durban by November. Many of the other yachts would be stopping first at Rodrigues, a small island 320 miles east of Mauritius. We had said no, in part because we didn't have any detailed charts of Rodrigues.

Before leaving Cocos-Keeling, the yachts that were heading the same way all decided to stay in touch via SSB radio at 8:00 a.m. and 4:00 p.m., Cocos-Keeling time. One of the yachts had no SSB radio and would be the source of a strange happening about 1,700 miles down the road.

Once back at sea, and after the usual adjustment, the days passed, and we quickly tuned in again to the sun and moon. There was the usual mal de mer, then it was soon gone and I could become part of TIGGER and our universe, which stretched a few miles in each direction horizontally, five or so miles down, and upward to infinity. How I love the heavens. I discovered that while the sea has captivated me, the heavens seen and experienced at sea are what have so completely captured my soul. My spirit is at its best out there.

There is a kind of loneliness in this awareness of where I belong. I miss my family when I am at sea, but they don't belong out there with me. Dave is my heart's companion, and he does belong at sea with me, but I am alone in this. Most of the time, life at sea is fairly normal—whatever that is. And then one night while I'm on watch, I'll just happen to look up at the stars and for a split second, I become part of them, fused with the universe, perfect and knowing all things, peaceful beyond words. Then it's gone, and I am human again, although that sublime split-second, coming now and again, will be enough to make all the minutes and hours and days in between worthwhile. I have actually had that experience a few times, at first in dreams, always on a windswept hill, and now on the ocean. I can't explain it. I sort of feel like I've met aliens and they're friendly! Actually, there is nothing light-hearted about it—it is a deep and profound feeling.

One night while alone on watch with a full-moon out I noticed that the sky was getting blacker and the stars brighter and more plentiful. All this was on a subconscious level, so I didn't stick my head out from under the awning to question the state of the sky. But finally, it was too pronounced to ignore, and I looked around the awning just in time to see a full eclipse of the moon. I didn't know it was to happen that night, and I hadn't checked the almanac since the GPS was tracking our position for us. But there it was, eerie and mystical, a black sky with bright stars all around the dull golden-brown circle that was the moon. By the time I looked, there was only a small sliver of yellow moon left and then even that disappeared. In that moment, I understood why the ancients gave sacrifices and both feared and worshiped the heavens. Dave got up to gaze at it, too, and then took over on his watch while I stayed up on deck to make sure everything returned to normal. Before it did, however, while the moon was still completely covered by the shadow of the earth, a very thick mist covered the sky and soon the moon and stars were obliterated.

The next night when it was time for the moon to rise, I was a wee bit apprehensive. Sure, I knew the moon would rise, but still a small voice inside my head kept saying, "Will the moon appear tonight. Is it still there in the heavens?" Of course it did rise, and all was well.

About 10 days out of Cocos-Keeling, we started talking about the possibility of stopping at Rodrigues after all. We'd found a hand-drawn chart of the entry to the anchorage in one of our cruising bulletins, and on our daily radio net, the folks on yachts ahead of us offered to give us the GPS coordinates and visual landmarks we would need to negotiate the reef and narrow channel. We often started out planning to bypass islands but almost always ended up stopping at the first land we came to. After many days of only the sea and sky, and long night watches, it was hard to resist the thought of a safe anchorage and a good night's sleep. Also, curiosity is strong in both of us, and the lure of a new, strange place is hard to resist. For me, it has been a force all my life. The sun setting on the horizon, and knowing that it is shining on another place, always draws me on.

Like many cruisers, when I am at sea I dream a lot. Actually, I have always had a very active dream life. But I loved my dreams at sea, and often woke up laughing at the crazy things I had just dreamed. I had one dream from which I awoke with my teeth hurting. Then I remembered that I had just dreamed that a huge hamburger had floated by me, and I had tried to take a big bite out of it. It was my jaws snapping on thin air that had awakened me!

Just a few days out of Rodrigues, I was ready to go on the afternoon radio schedule with the other yachts. We had not seen another ship for days, but knew, because of our daily radio contact, that there were three yachts ahead of us and at least one behind. In all our passages, we always kept the VHF radio on and tuned to channel 16. If we saw a ship, we would call and if by chance it actually answered, would ask if they had seen us on their radar. It was always reassuring when they answered and told us that they did, indeed, see us. It was even better when they told us that they had seen us on radar before we'd called. I once had quite a chat with a young Egyptian officer who answered my call. He told me about his experience of getting shot at in Houston. Good old Texas, good old USA! He did say that a taxi driver had stopped and gotten him out of the danger. He must have quite an impression of Texas.

On this particular day, I heard a ship calling someone on the VHF radio. Initially, the signal kept breaking up, but I figured it was within 20 miles or so, since that is our usual range on the VHF. After several minutes, however, I realized he was calling a yacht, telling the "yacht in distress" that he was on his way to rescue them. That got my attention! KULLA II, a

Swedish yacht, was about 10 miles ahead of us, and since it was time for the SSB net, I called and asked them if they could hear the transmissions. They couldn't, and I now had both radios going, the SSB to talk to Gunnar on KULLA II, and the VHF to listen to the M/V COMANCHE talking to the boat in distress. I continued to listen to the one-sided conversation, and with a sinking heart thought I heard the name of the yacht behind us, belonging to a couple from Switzerland. Moments later, however, I finally made out that COMANCHE was on its way to respond to an EPIRB (Emergency Position Indicating Radio Beacon) signal from the yacht YAO, the one without the SSB. I repeatedly tried to call the ship. Did they need us to stand by or to help them with the distressed yacht? But they didn't answer my call, and I couldn't tell where they were. I knew they were within our range somewhere, but which way? Were we near the yacht YAO? Could we help? Should we stop, turn around, sail a search pattern? I felt very helpless. It is such a huge ocean, and we were so small. As I listened some more, I heard the captain of the COMANCHE as he approached the yacht, and then again as they got alongside and had the rescue harnesses on the two people onboard the yacht. The last I heard was the captain telling them to make sure their harnesses were tight, and that they were about to be hauled up. Of course, after that they could talk face to face, no need for VHF communications and no more eavesdropping for me.

It was a very unsettling feeling, knowing that near us a yacht was sinking. The day was gentle, with light winds and fairly flat seas. What happened? How fragile we are out there. No violent storm sunk them. What went wrong?

The next day I called Tony's net in Kenya and asked if he had heard of an EPIRB going off in our area. He said no, but that he would call Cape Town, South Africa, the rescue center for the Indian Ocean, and check. Just then another voice came on the radio, a captain of another freighter, and he offered to call right then, reporting back about 30 minutes later that the reason the EPIRB call was not common knowledge was because it was only on for about an hour. That's when CO-MANCHE had heard the distress call, which had been relayed from Cape Town. This captain even talked to the captain of the rescue ship. The captain of the COMANCHE reported that the crew was safe and well, and that the ship was proceeding to Richards Bay, South Africa. The yacht, however, had not been scuttled, so we all had to be on the lookout for a half-submerged yacht, not a pleasant thought in the dark. When I asked for the location of the rescue, it turned out to be 90 miles away. No wonder COMANCHE had never heard us. How in the world did we hear them? VHF is line of sight, and the antennas on freighters are pretty high, but still, 90 miles away? It was all very strange and weird, and since we didn't get to South Africa for many weeks, we never did learn what actually happened to cause the sinking. One more mystery.

24

Land of the Dodo Birds

On the 17th day, we sighted the island of Rodrigues and made our way to the GPS waypoints we'd recently received over the radio, since the yacht HARLEQUIN had gone in before us and given us directions and landmarks. So with our little hand-drawn chart and those instructions, we made landfall; in daylight, of course. Rodrigues is a possession of Mauritius, so we put on clothes and raised the flag of Mauritius. Since we knew nothing about this island, we had no accompanying song or motto.

The entrance channel is narrow and shallow, but well-marked, with coral visible on each side. The anchorage is in front of the town, and it's quite small and surrounded by coral. We managed to raft up to another yacht at the pier to get checked in, then moved into the anchorage. All the yachts there, however, had been warned they would have to move when the supply ship came in since it needed lots of room to maneuver.

A chance encounter with an unusual person that first day made my stay in Rodrigues very special. We were walking back to the dock when I saw two ladies in white saris. They were slowly walking along the dock, and as we were about to pass, one asked, "Are you from one of the yachts?"

"Yes," I replied. She told me her name was Sangita and that she wanted to welcome us to Rodrigues. She went on to tell us that they, too, were visiting and that they were both from Mauritius and on Rodrigues to teach meditation and yoga to the women of the island. Then she asked, "Would you like to hear more about yoga?"

Since I had immediately sensed something special about these women (the other woman stood silently while the first one talked), I said, "Yes, I would like that very much," even though Dave had by this time backed away, quite skeptical about such things. The two women and I ultimately agreed to meet on the dock the next night at 6 o'clock. I was told I could invite any other cruisers who might be interested.

Picture this, eight yachties sitting on benches at the end of a covered jetty. Standing in front of us, giving us a gentle lecture on positive thinking is a beautiful Hindu lady in a white sari. Her voice was heavily accented, but lilting and sweet. Outside our small group, the rain was coming down, and the wind was blowing in the dark night. All the yachties who said they would come did so, and I really had to marvel at this unique experience in the middle of the Indian Ocean. It took a while before it dawned on me that she was a Hindu missionary! When she was done, she asked if anyone would like to meet the next night, and, though we all agreed only a young Brazilian and I showed up.

I was fascinated by Sangita's story of creation and the "eye." It reminded me very much of what Christian missionaries must teach to "heathens" about Jesus and God—very simple, but very powerful. We met each night for the next four nights, and though in the end, I was the only one, I felt quite touched by the missionaries' concern for my spirit. They were spending their time with me after a busy day of working with the women of Rodrigues.

One lesson particularly stood out, as it represented to me how very different our understanding of the world is. One evening she said in one of her examples of patience, "Suppose your maid did something really wrong, like broke a special dish. Your first desire may be to beat your maid. You may be very angry, but if you pause for a moment, you will see that a beating will not solve anything. Then you will be able to calm yourself and instruct your maid in the right way to do things." Maids, beatings? We *were* from different cultures! Yet the lesson of patience was there, and sincere and real. I started out thinking I would get one lesson in yoga, and ended up understanding I should not beat my maid. It surely did my heart good.

The three-day trip to Mauritius was rough, with irregular waves and the wind absolutely behind us, so that we were rolling the whole way. I had thought my mal de mer was clearing up, but no, I was seasick every minute so all I remember is the misery!

Mauritius was another place I had heard of all my life, and now here we were. We sailed into Port Louis to check in, intending to leave immediately and go 10 miles up the coast to Grand Baie. But since there were a half dozen yachts that had all arrived within 12 hours of each other, things got a little complicated, especially since the Customs and Immigration officials were both easygoing and a little disorganized. In the end they went to one yacht, and we all gathered there for stamps and initials. We had heard more than a few warnings about Port Louis thievery, and one of the yachties just checking in had several small items stolen even as they stepped off the boat to get fresh water. Jim, the skipper, was apologetic, saying that it was his fault for leaving these fellows on his boat. But I guess to me stealing is stealing, and the victim is not the bad guy. Oh well, we headed for Grand Baie as soon as we could.

Mauritius is about 35 miles long and 25 miles wide, the island where early explorers managed to kill all the dodo birds in less than 100 years. These were peculiar-looking, flightless birds, and not afraid of strangers with weapons. They probably tasted good too. The sailors of old were not as ecology-minded as we are today. Too bad. I would have loved to see one in the wild and not just as drawings in old books.

The coastal land is flat, but rises to the most awesome spires inland. Grand Baie is a perfect anchorage, sheltered and shallow. I was still sick from the trip, which was unusual, since I normally felt fine as soon as we got into calm water. A few days later I realized I had picked up another virus, so I spent most of the 10 days that we were there resting on the boat. Still, I had a wonderful view of those grand spires, and the few trips I did make to town were pleasant with no worries about personal safety beyond the usual tourist cautions.

We left Mauritius from Port Louis again since all yachts had to go back there to check out. This time though, no docking was allowed at the new customs dock and hotel complex, and it was back to an old grainery with loading spouts projecting from its seaward walls. Departing yachts were rafted three deep at the dock, and it was dangerous, dirty and irritating to have to go there when a new and safer dock was available. The reason the new dock was being kept empty was that it was awaiting a group of rally boats. This one was going around the world in just a year or so, and the organizer was setting everything up for the group in each country so that all they had to do was sail in, look around and then sail on. These boats were all big, expensive and fast. And though they still had 10 days before they would be in Mauritius, the dock was closed to us.

When I took our lines from our neighbor in preparation for motoring away from the dock, the engine died. I handed our dock lines back and that was that. The rest of that day, I fretted while Dave tried to find the problem. It turned out to be the fuel pump, which he changed the next morning, and we slipped out of Port Louis before port control could question why we had stayed the day before when we were supposed to go.

Passing by the French island of Réunion, I had my fishing line out, trolling again, since we were near shore and I was hoping for a lucky strike that day. I had decided to use my prize lure, a $25 purple feather squid that I'd only used once because it was so pretty and did not like salt water, and well, I never caught anything anyway. This time, just 10 minutes after I put the line out, I got a strike. But grabbing the hand line, I felt a pull and then a snap as the line broke, and moments later I saw a huge tuna in the distance, leaping high out of the water with my beautiful purple lure dangling from its mouth. I packed my fishing gear away, said a not so gentle goodbye to my lure and the tuna, and settled down for our long passage to Durban. Clothes stayed on this time as we were heading for higher latitudes.

25

✑

Let the Winds Blow—Harder

Conventional cruising wisdom states that you should go about 120 miles south of the island of Madagascar as you make your way to South Africa, since there is a continental shelf off that coast. When the winds from the South Indian Ocean blow up that way, it can be very treacherous. Also, if you stay south, you may be able to pick up the nice west-setting current that flows toward Africa and then joins the south-flowing Agulhas Current that runs down the coast of Africa and around the Cape. We are a cautious pair, and even though staying far south of Madagascar added some miles to the passage, we plotted our course with that information in mind.

We were now in that part of the Indian Ocean where you can feel the effects of the weather patterns forming in the South Atlantic and funneling around the Cape. It was October, and the days were often squally, dark and bumpy. As we rounded Madagascar, we relished the idea of that west-setting current giving us a push. But it never came. And in fact, we managed to find the countercurrent so that our speed was slowed by at least a knot for several days. This was contrary to everything we had read and heard. But when I talked to Alistair, our Ham radio contact in South Africa for weather, he merely said, "Oh yes, sometimes there is a countercurrent. Fancy that you caught it."

Still, the days went by, the miles passed beneath the keel and South Africa kept getting closer. Africa, the Dark Continent: How I had always wanted to say that—because of the mystery, of the region's ancient and dark history. Imagine, from Egypt, with Cleopatra, Luxor and the Nile, to the steamy jungles of central Africa then all the way to the diamond mines of South Africa, and safaris and big white hunters. How can you say the word Namibia without thinking of isolated outposts of civilization, vast savannas and giant sand dunes shifting down to the Atlantic Ocean? Even today, the countries are constantly changing and shifting, and through all the poverty and brutal dictatorships, there is still a call of adventure. Power and intrigue seem to be a mainstay of this resource-rich continent, and I was going to see it.

At noon on the 13th day out we had only 90 miles to the coast and were trying to time it all so that we would make landfall during daylight. A close look at the Durban chart showed a very narrow channel leading into the harbor. And in fact, in Grand Baie, a neighbor who had sailed many times to Durban, told us that only one ship could go through the channel at a time. If a freighter was exiting the channel, we would have to stand off and let it come out before we would be permitted to enter. He made it sound very busy, bustling and nerve-wracking. So 90 miles at noon meant a morning entry on the next day—perfect.

There was one more concern about nearing the coast of South Africa—a concern more anxiety provoking than the harbor entrance—and that was the weather. I had already read much about the "Cape of Storms," in accounts written by everyone from Captain Cook to present-day cruisers. Of course, weather was inevitably the dominant subject. Apparently at this time of the year there was a tendency for lows to form in the South Atlantic, head east to South Africa, roll around the Cape and then blow up the east coast. An additional consideration was the effect of the Agulhas Current, which is swift and in some places 90 miles wide. It flows down the Mozambique Channel, between Madagascar and mainland Africa, then around Cape Agulhas before dissipating into the Southern Atlantic. Of course, the swiftest part of the current was near Durban!

As a result there were two things to keep in mind as we approached Durban. First, could we sneak in before a southwest "buster," as the worst of the lows are called, came rolling up the coast producing what have been described by some as the most dangerous waves in the world? And then, how would we sail across this swift current without being swept past Durban and forced to make our way back up the coast?

It sounded tricky, and we checked with Alistair every day on the radio weather net, picked up weather faxes several times a day and hoped for good luck. We were nervous and didn't talk to each other much during those days getting closer to Africa. A friend once said that what she loved best about quitting her job and going sailing was that she had time to slow down and think. But now, we were both far too focused on making a landfall in one piece to have anytime for daydreaming.

That day, Alistair told us that our timing looked good, that there didn't seem to be any lows coming around the Cape and that there would be northeast winds 15–20 knots and moderate seas. That meant the wind and seas were off our starboard quarter—behind us, as they had been for the past 24 hours. The sky was clear, with white puffy clouds flying past overhead, driven by some faster wind high above us. Ninety miles at 5 knots was 18 hours, perfect for a morning landfall. Great, perfect, good landfall. We were happy.

Two hours later, after we had told Alistair we would call him from Durban the next day to let him know we'd made it, the wind went from 20 to 25 knots and kept rising. We had already reefed the main but had a good piece of jib out. I was on deck and anxiously waiting for my watch to end. With the wind rising, the motion of the boat was getting increasingly uncomfortable. But I didn't want to wake up Dave as he was going to need all the rest he could get before the final approach to Durban. Every now and then a wave would roll up on our starboard quarter, and TIGGER would first rise, then heel severely as she slid down the side of the wave and crashed into the trough as the wave flattened out. TIGGER would then twist around as the wind steering tried to get us back on course. Like a galloping horse that trips and struggles to regain its footing, TIGGER was using every muscle to recover, and I was straining along with her. In fact the boat was out of control, and I didn't like it! May be the sails were not balanced, may be there was too much sail up, may be the wrong sails were up, but TIGGER was not moving well through the water and that was a bad thing for both her and us. Finally, anxiety nibbling at my nerves, I woke Dave, who grumbled as I explained that we were being blown off the waves, and that there was too much sail up, and the wind steering couldn't recover, and I was uncomfortable: yak, yak, yak, nag, nag, nag. I assured him that if we put up the trysail and staysail, we would move better, the wind steering would be able to keep us on course, and I would quit nagging. "Oh, by the way, we're beginning to move too fast."

Meanwhile the wind continued to rise, still out of the northeast, still behind us, so Dave got up and together we lowered the main, put up the trysail, rolled in the jib and decided we didn't need the staysail and that did the trick. TIGGER now took the waves like the thoroughbred she was, and we steadily moved through the waves in a controlled and powerful manner. I forgot to be anxious; I was exhilarated! In the next two hours, the wind reached 55 knots apparent, and we were sailing at 7 knots with that one little sail. It was still a lovely, clear day, with puffy clouds and deep blue sky. But the seas were now big with spray blowing off the tops as they crumbled under their own weight. I had already donned foulweather gear, and this time even put on boots. Normally, I would have only put on a jacket to keep the wind from giving me too much of a chill. But we were now in the higher latitudes where the water and air were too cold for such casual behavior.

It now appeared it was going to blow 45 to 55 knots for a while, which meant that although TIGGER was under control, we were approaching the coast so fast we would make landfall before daylight. But heave-to? Stand off until morning? Not this time, for we were now well within the current and fast being swept south. Our course had us far enough north of Durban to account for our drift if we kept moving, but not if we were to stop. In fact, we would never get across the current that way. There was also the question of whether this northeast gale would be replaced by a southwest buster, something that was entirely possible along this coast. It was too horrible to contemplate. TIGGER had no choice. We would have to find some way to get safely into Durban Harbor in a 50-knot gale with high seas, a narrow channel and in darkness.

Anyone who has ever approached a city at night from the sea knows how frustrating it is to try to pick out one red and one green light marking the entrance to a harbor. The city sky-

Warming up after a gale, off the South African coast

line is full of red and green neon lights, dozens of other bright pinpoints of light and radio tower lights all seemingly designed to frustrate and confuse. We saw the loom of Durban, then the lights of the coast. Oh, how I had dreamed of this day—Africa! But now, I was dreading closing with land, illogically straining my eyes for something identifiable long before it was possible.

It began to look like a midnight landfall, maybe 1 a.m. Through all the tension of trying to get our bearings, there was still the thrill of feeling TIGGER moving through the wild sea, trysail tight, the wind steering holding us steady on our course. All concentration goes to the boat and to the sea. No casual navigation now. Down the companionway, check the chart, check the GPS and plot our position. Does it fit with what we can make out of the coast? Can we trust the GPS? What if the chart is wrong? What if the GPS is off? What if there are some rocks or shallows not marked on the chart? Is that a ship coming out? Is the wind getting higher? Stop it! Don't even think about inviting those kinds of thoughts to this party.

Around 10 p.m., Dave took over and I went below to see if I could rest for a while. But Dave soon had me up again to check the chart. The night was a moonless black, the city lights glaring and smearing into one another through the spray of the waves. As we got closer to shore, the waves were no longer quite so high, but they felt steeper and harsher. One came up on the starboard quarter, crested right against the weather cloth and tore it from its lashing, leaving it flapping in the wind. The cockpit filled with water. That was a first. In all our miles, that had never happened.

By the time we were close to shore, we had another surprise: ships, lots of them. They were anchored near the channel, riding out the gale, waiting to go in. We would come up on a wave, see a silhouette of a ship against the glare of city lights, and then down we would go, lost in total blackness in the trough of the wave. Concentrate, concentrate! As we came up on a wave, I would scan for anchored ships near us or in our path while Dave concentrated on holding TIGGER both on course and safe in these steep waves. Down we would go, and the world would disappear. Up we would rise, and I would scan the city with the binoculars looking for where I thought the channel should be.

I am not an especially patient person, and by this time the anxiety was not just nibbling, but taking bites out of my nerves. My frustration was nearing panic when suddenly I had an epiphany, a thought that settled in quickly but gently and promptly seemed to put everything in perspective. "Sharon, the waves will not lay down so you can see, and you cannot just brush them aside. The wind will not calm because you need to go slower and take your time. The other lights will not go out in the city so you can find your lights. The sky will not brighten so you can see your surroundings better. It just won't happen. They don't know you are here. They don't care. And that is the nature of nature!"

It was a simple concept, and in the flurry of nerves, a bit hard to accept. But then the thought became my reality, and I was suddenly alive. Truly, really, alive. It's hard to explain, but I was part of it all—the wind, the dark night, the sharp, jerking seas. My consciousness shifted somehow, and I was aware of it even as it happened. Now I could hold the glasses a little steadier, patiently let the wave obliterate my view and wait for the next clearing. Scan, drop to darkness, rise on a wave, dodge the ship in our path, scan some more.

We knew from our GPS position that we were close to the harbor channel, and the city lights were close, as was the coast. But where were the breakwater lights marking the entrance? One red, keep that one to port. It's "red left return" in this part of the world. One green light, keep that one to starboard. The south jetty was the longest, jutting farther out from land; that was to protect the harbor from the waves stirred up by the southwest busters—bigger, meaner and more dangerous. But now the wind was northeast so the waves would be driving right down the channel. About three miles out, I called Port Control. They sit in a tower on a cliff high above the channel and have an excellent view of the area. I told them we were coming in and we couldn't stop for traffic coming out, for the seas were too rough. And by the way, how was the channel? Calm?

"No, not really, it's pretty rough I would say," came the reply. Great. Could they see us? Were we anywhere near the channel entrance? "Not to worry," the operator said. "No ships are leaving tonight, come on in. And yes, we can see you on course for the channel."

Somewhere in that control tower, a calm South African knew we were there, making our way to safe harbor in this gale. That was a great comfort.

I was back in the cockpit when Port Control called and said, "Do you see the red light of the jetty?" But I didn't answer because I was too busy searching. Then, before I could see any kind of light, I saw the waves crashing on the jetty in question. What a fright! I was sure we were close, way too close. For some time now Dave and I had been shouting to each other to be heard, which was mostly futile because of the howling wind. Now I screamed at Dave, "Go to starboard, to starboard, hurry, the rocks." After which TIGGER began turning to starboard, and I heard Dave shout, "I see the rocks, and I see the red and green lights, and we've got lots of room." Then we were surfing through the channel entrance and suddenly we were in flat water. He was calm, the crazy guy! Just like that, we were out of the waves.

Port Control had told us to go to the customs dock, a small boat basin just inside the entrance, so I hurried forward to bring down the trysail while Dave motored to where he thought the dock was. The wind was still 45 knots, but the water was flat so maneuvering was easier—not easy, just easier. We passed by the dock while Port Control was telling us over the radio to, "Turn, turn," and we did a Keystone Kops routine until we could find the entrance to the basin. There were several large fishing boats tied up, and the wind was pushing us around a bit. I got out the docklines and fenders to protect us from the concrete walls of the basin. Out of the night, a man appeared on the dock—a security guard, not a sailor—but he was there to help, and he took our lines and held them tight around a dock cleat until we could get TIGGER close by and in control. It took some doing to get tied up with the wind trying to push TIGGER into a steel fishing boat. Dave poured on the power to miss it, and another fellow appeared on the dock to take our second line.

At last we were tied up, and thanked the men for their help. They told us that customs would be around at 7 o'clock that morning. It was 2 a.m. Imagine that, we were in Africa. And in one piece! Dave said it was time for a drink. I said, "I think I will cry instead, thank you very much." Both good tension relievers. He had his drink, I had my cry, and we slept our first night on the Dark Continent.

26

✍

Talking to the Animals, Kruger National Park

The Point Yacht Club is in the heart of Durban. As we pulled into the International Jetty, which is reserved for visiting yachts, Bob Fraser, longtime member and leader at the club, came by to greet us as he has been doing with visiting yachts for many, many years. He gave us a good overview of the places in the city to visit and also the general atmosphere of the city and country via his own history and feelings about the changes in South Africa.

We had waited all morning for Customs and Immigration, but nobody had shown up at the small boat basin where we'd been instructed to stop, which is why we had proceeded to the yacht club. Dave checked with the club office, and they duly called customs, which reported that we could go ashore and that they would come to us when they could. It was two weeks before we were officially checked into the country! But no one seemed to care or worry about it, so we didn't either. There were about 10 other foreign yachts at the same dock, and they had all experienced this sort of delay with no difficulties in the end, so we settled down, relaxed and started to look around.

South Africa is an astoundingly beautiful country. Except for Durban and Cape Town, the only big cities we saw, the country seemed about 50 years behind the United States— harsher perhaps, but simpler and cleaner than life often is today. Whether they were black or white, British, Afrikaner or Indian, the people we met seemed to love their country fiercely. But talk to a white person, and they would despair of the country ever coming right; while from a black person you would hear a lot of hope, mixed with cynicism about the government's ability to keep its promises. It made my heart ache to think that South Africa may go the way of so many other countries in Africa—corrupt leaders, desperate poverty for most of its citizens and vast wealth for the powerful few. I don't know how it will all turn out, but they have so much worth working for. I hope all of them, leaders and ordinary citizens, do the right thing, and I wish them well.

Crime seemed the biggest threat. The first night we were there, the night guard at the yacht club was murdered. The third night, a man was shot and killed by the police, while hiding in the water among the yachts—he had tried to rob a restaurant. After that, things around our neighborhood seemed to settle down, although we were always careful as to where and when we walked through town, and the yacht club secretary told me not to look so much like a tourist. I wasn't sure how not to look like what I was.

My big desire was to go to a game park, and after a few false starts, we hooked up with a fellow named Peter Westermann, who runs a company called Zebra Tours and specializes in Kruger National Park and the surrounding private game parks. We made arrangements for him to be our guide and he picked us up at the yacht club in his Land Rover, drove us to Kruger, then drove us through the park to game watch during the day.

While on the way, we passed through Swaziland, a small country set in the northeast part of South Africa. We checked into Swaziland at 10 a.m., drove to the other end of the country and checked out at 11:00 a.m. Then we resumed our drive in South Africa to Kruger.

We had just come through the park gates and started the 30-mile drive to Skukuza where we would make base, when suddenly Peter stopped the Land Rover and pointed. There was a lioness strolling alongside the road, paying no attention to us. I didn't realize how loose-jointed a lion is. She just slung along so easily, but with such strength. What a sight. Just then Peter said excitedly, "Look on the other side." And there was another lioness, only this one had cubs with her. We started counting them as they tumbled and played behind her. We stopped when we reached 12. Twelve cubs—it's impossible for one lioness to have that many cubs and Peter was beside himself with wonder and joy. He said he had never seen that. Sometimes one lioness will baby-sit while another is hunting, but 12 cubs is a record. And we were just barely inside the park!

Kruger Park belongs to the animals—it's their home, not a zoo—and we were the ones in the cage at night. Skukuza is the main camp in the approximately 8,000-square-mile park, and Peter had arranged for a "luxury" tent facing the perimeter of the camp. The gates closed promptly at 6 p.m. and didn't open again until 6 o'clock in the morning. So you had better be inside the gates on time or plan to sleep with the lions.

Peter got us settled, his tent next to ours, and then we picked up some groceries at the camp store. Peter provided breakfast, but we bought lunch at one of several rest stops in the park, and in the evening, we shared provisions, which he cooked over the grill. Peter told us these were his favorite tents in the camp, and he always requested them because at dusk we would see the hyenas as they prowled the perimeter of the camp. Sure enough, along they came that evening, looking like dogs, except for their sloping backs and powerful jaws. They would come through the bush, stop at the fence and sometimes lay down in front of us like dogs lounging in front of a fireplace. What surprised me most about the hyenas was how healthy they looked. Their coats were not scruffy and dull like a zoo animal's, but sleek and clean. I knew these fellows were often fed through the fence by the visitors. It was absolutely forbidden, but it was done, so they came back each night.

Other than that instance I never once saw an animal acting like a domestic animal or one in a zoo. The rest were wild and true to their real natures. In Kruger, the byword is "hands off." If an animal is sick, it gets well on its own or dies. There are scavengers to clean its carcass. Every creature has a place in this cycle, and it was our privilege at last to see animals as nature intended. Even the dung beetles have an important role, and when a beetle crossed the road, cars stopped for them for they are too precious to the ecology of the park to damage. These little insects collect the dung of animals, roll it into manageable balls, roll the balls to their nests and lay their eggs in it. When the babies hatch, they have both a home and food to sustain them until they can leave and repeat the process. Thus, even excrement is useful. Everything is needed and has a purpose. I never want to go to a zoo again. This experience gave me another level of respect for this incredible planet we live on.

One day, we were on the road when some elephants came crashing through the bush and started crossing in front of us. Peter quickly stopped the car and commented that elephants made him more nervous than lions. They are so big and unpredictable. He had seen an elephant stomp a Land Rover before they could even back up and get away, and the people had just barely escaped. The Rover was a ruin. Though Peter had turned our engine off, he had his hand on the ignition and was ready to start up and back away if needed. As we sat there, more and more adult elephants came out of the bush in single file to cross the road. Following them, came the juveniles. One large male elephant stopped at the side of the road as if he were a crossing guard. He looked at us; we looked at him; he started to flap his ears and swing his trunk. Peter was getting more nervous by the minute, knowing the signs of stress in the animal. He was talking very quietly to us, and both Dave and I were stunned at the scene before us. Finally, in the interest of safety, Peter started the Rover and backed up just a bit. About that same time, the children were across and so were the last of the adults. The guard tossed his trunk and ambled off into the bush, and all three of us sighed in relief. We had counted 30 elephants. I was thrilled beyond words.

Then Peter said, "Let's go meet them at the watering hole. I know that is where they are going." And with that, he took off along a dusty, dirt side road, back into the bush to a circle turnaround next to two small ponds. There we stopped and waited quietly for the elephants to arrive. Sure enough, soon we heard the crashing brush, and there they were!

The juveniles headed for the pools and immediately began splashing in the water, scooping up water in their trunk and tossing it on their backs. We were laughing and talking, and I was trying to decide if I could get a good picture, when suddenly two huge male elephants appeared on the road leading

Adult elephant escorting a young one across Kruger National Park, South Africa

back out, tramping towards us. When elephants are in the movies or the *National Geographic* Magazine, they don't look half as big as when they are lumbering down the road toward you. The whole scene seemed unreal, like we were in a movie. I was getting nervous because Peter was getting nervous. If that was part of his "give the tourists a show" act, he was really good at it. Finally, the giants left the road, and we started breathing again. My breathing had now been seriously interrupted several times during our encounter with the elephants.

Another stop was an escarpment that rose about 1,000 feet above a broad valley that stretched away for many, many miles below us. This was a scene of the real Africa. A scene before man had changed the landscape to fit his needs. A river ran through the valley, and there was every manner of animal. Hippo, giraffe, zebra, rhino, warthog, impala, wildebeest, elephant—they were all down there. We gazed through our binoculars for an hour, capturing this fantastic vision forever in our memories.

Another day, a leopard had killed an impala and hauled its carcass into a tree. He tore off a haunch and brought it to the bottom of the tree to feast. This was right beside the road, and we stopped and watched. When the leopard finished, he got up and walked past our Land Rover as if we weren't even there. There was no fear, for this was his country.

Peter was a wonderful guide, tall and blonde and smiling. A transplant from Holland, he had come to South Africa to work 20 years earlier, because he hadn't known what he wanted to do with his life. He'd fallen in love with Kruger, and had been guiding tourists ever since. He loved the park, and it showed in his enthusiasm and knowledge of the animals and birds.

Oh, the birds! Since Dave is an avid birder, and I am an enthusiastic novice, we especially enjoyed the birds. The weaverbird is a small, bright yellow bird that builds a nest that is shaped like a teardrop. The nests are made out of twigs that the male collects and weaves to make his home. When he is done, the female inspects the nest and if she approves, she moves in and they mate. If she doesn't—well, he has to start all over. One day I was watching close to a hundred nests in a big tree when two birds caught my interest because of their behavior. They were busy weaving. When one finished with his twig and left to collect another, the other bird would go to his nest, take the twig he had just placed and bring it back and weave it into his own nest. Back came the honest bird to weave his new twig and then fly off to get another. Again, the thief stole the twig and put it into his nest. This went on all the time I was watching. Didn't the honest bird ever realize that his nest was not getting any bigger, while the neighbor's nest was growing nicely? I laughed for a long time over that, and it still makes me smile.

We could have stayed for weeks at Kruger, watching the animals and letting Peter do the cooking, but money dictates. In the end, our private tour cost about what we estimated we would have spent if we had rented a car, driving ourselves and arranging our own hotels and meals. Whatever the cost, it was well worth it. The game park is one of the highlights of my sightseeing life.

Later I flew back to Texas for Christmas, while Dave stayed with TIGGER in Durban. It was time for some new bottom paint and stainless steel work, and Durban was a good place to effect repairs. The exchange rate was excellent and so was the work done there.

27

❧

Rounding the Cape

It is always stormy in the southern oceans. But some times are worse than others. Luckily we would be rounding the tip of Africa in the Southern Hemisphere's summer and we'd also have the Agulhas Current to help us along. Still what about those lows coming around from the South Atlantic? South-setting current meets southwesterly wind. If the wind is strong enough, that equals "the most dangerous waves in the world." Remember? And the lows don't come up the coast at 10 knots, but rather at 25 knots, 35 knots or higher. I loved saying, "the most dangerous waves in the world," when sitting in a quiet, safe anchorage in some other ocean. But saying it when about to head out into the Agulhas Current, now that sent a shiver down my spine! As it turns out, Cape Agulhas, not the Cape of Good Hope, is the southern tip of Africa. The Cape of Good Hope is actually 60 miles up the coast on the western side, so Agulhas was our goal.

I think all the foreign yachts in Durban were feeling some trepidation about the upcoming leg. And the Ocean Sailing School, which was based near the yacht club and provided sessions on the logic of planning the trip, always had a full house when it came time to round the Cape. The key was to sail out into the fast-moving southerly current and head quickly from port to port, all the time keeping an eye out for any changes in the weather and never letting yourself get out too far. There are good, safe ports along the south coast to duck into, but the conditions can turn so quickly, you can get caught out. What to look for was a weather window that allowed you to make the next port only. If, by chance, the weather got nasty, you were to head directly to shore. *Directly.* If you could get close to shore, and out of the current, you could escape the killer waves and only have a gale to deal with. Our instructors were full of cautions, and some of the local sailors said they were more cautious than necessary. But we all felt we needed to know as much as possible, and even overly-ominous warnings were necessary, to our minds. Talking about the waves would send shimmers of anxiety through me. But still, it was all exciting and hard to believe that we were here at the bottom of Africa, getting ready to do what sailors had been doing for hundreds of years: face the Cape of Storms. I always felt the romance of the adventure.

As the time to leave approached, each day, morning and afternoon, we would trek to the sailing school. There we would look at weather faxes, listen to the advice of the instructors, talk among ourselves, and then make up our minds whether it was go or no go. The instructor's advice held a lot of weight.

One day at the morning briefing he said, "I don't think today is good, there is a very short window before the next low." But then in the afternoon he said, "Hey, it looks like today is good after all, you may have up to 36 hours to make East London." And a number of us got ready to go. There were about 10 boats in all and most of them took off at 5 p.m. to sail all night towards East London, 240 miles down the coast. But Dave was hesitating (should we, shouldn't we) and after we threw off the dock lines he suddenly changed his mind and said we would set out the following day.

The next morning we left later than we had planned. How did we oversleep when we were so jittery? It was full daylight as we motored out through the choppy channel and put up the reefed main and rolled out a bit of jib. We had northeast winds, 20 to 25 knots, as we headed out looking for the current. But since we were moving southeast instead of east, and not directly out to the current, it took us 70 miles before we could feel its effects. Then suddenly we were going 10 knots! We planned to keep on the side of the current closest to land so we could make a break for the shore if the wind shifted against us.

It was strange having a light anxiety as our constant companion. The sailing was great, but we kept glancing to the southwest. At the sailing school they had posted photos of a sky that went from clear blue to a black gale in less than 10 minutes, unbelievable but true. For the moment, though, we were still moving fast, averaging 10 knots with a reefed main and half jib.

Alas, but our window had narrowed too quickly, and about 16 hours after we left, the wind shifted to the southwest. It had died several hours before, and we'd started motoring, knowing that something was coming. In fact, we were already heading for shore when it shifted around. Luckily, it was not 50 knots, just 20 to 25. We tried to stay about a mile offshore where the seas were calm, and we only had to contend with motorsailing and short tacking into these headwinds. We were making very slow progress and keeping a close eye on the rugged and isolated coast.

Finally the blow played itself out, and TIGGER ghosted into East London 38 hours after starting out, on a lovely moon-bright night, with us picking our way up the river that serves as a harbor, towards the visitors dock. We tied to the dock wall and slept well. We had made the longest passage between ports until the Cape. Now the ports were closer together, with 150 miles to our next stop, Port Elizabeth.

We spent 10 days at East London, while the southwest wind blew hard. Some days, the wind shifted to the southeast, but only a few hours later it was back to the southwest, not enough time to get to the next port. "Very unusual weather this year," was the locals' comment, but we had heard that before and smiled and nodded. We also got to see the first coelacanth (stuffed), which was brought up from the deep in the late 1930s off the coast of East London. The local museum chronicled the discovery and subsequent catches of this seriously ugly fish, which was once thought to have been extinct for millions of years. The museum also had a chart of all known shipwrecks around the Cape, and we counted about 200 since 1980. Yes, in just the past few years 200 ships had faced the Cape and lost. This was a sobering moment for me.

Soon afterwards the wind died and gave us a 24-hour window at 2 o'clock in the morning, and we untied and headed out to the current. This leg was 150 miles but with a great current, we could make it in less than 24 hours. We found the current quickly and also had a light following wind, so we were soon busting along at 12 knots with just the main up. The morning brought all sparkling water and a bright blue sky framed a golden sun. Glorious is the word I use for this kind of a day, no other word will do.

Unfortunately we were so busy enjoying the speed and the weather that we got a bit lax on the point at which we needed to start heading for the coast again. So we found ourselves too far south and had to motorsail against both wind and current to get back on track for the last 60 miles across the huge bay into Port Elizabeth. There was lots of lightning to the north of us that evening, and I was very thankful that the weather moves north along this coast. We tied up at midnight, with the help of several yacht club members who were wandering the docks after an evening at the bar. Two hours later, a 50-knot southwest buster hit! But we were tucked safely in the marina, and I hardly noticed the wildness in the night, except to send up a sleepy prayer of thanks.

Our next weather window came quickly, and we were only in Port Elizabeth for two days before moving on. Dave observed a sad and shocking incident while he was walking to the store, on a hill above the marina. In order to get there on foot, we had to cross a set of railroad tracks and go through some scrub to get to the road that led to the store. While Dave was crossing the railroad tracks, he passed a man beating a woman. There were other men around watching, but no one was helping the woman, who was in dire straits. Dave knew better than to intervene in fear for his own life, and he ran to the store and told them what was happening. They told him it happens all the time, and the police wouldn't even bother coming if they did call so they didn't. When he came home with that tale, I cried for a long time for the woman who had no protection. It's hard for me to talk about it even now.

Later, when Dave told an Afrikaner about it, the man calmly said, "Oh, they do that all the time. The women of that tribe like it, it shows their man loves them." How can I reconcile the charming helpful white people of South Africa with a statement like that? And how could I understand and empathize with the struggle of the black people of South Africa after what Dave saw? I don't know how. I also didn't like what the casual attitude toward violence was doing to me, not just in South Africa, but in our own country, too. In another town, we saw a man lying face down on the road, not moving. He was in the middle of the road—no cars traveled on it—but he was truly lying in the road. We thought he must be drunk and walked on by. When we came back that way, he was gone. Maybe he was drunk, but then again maybe he was hurt, sick or dead. We could have at least stopped and checked. The person I used to be would not have walked by. Remember what I said earlier about one person being good to one other person? I really missed on that one.

A day later we were at Port St. Francis, a small marina and resort development, or at least that had been their plan. As it was, the marina was only half-finished and the resort development was still on the drawing board. There were four other yachts waiting out the weather, and we were all there for seven days, on another wild and isolated coast. They were beautiful days, but a fierce wind blew out of the southwest.

Finally, we cast off lines and made our way to Mossel Bay, our last stop before rounding the Cape. A short walk through the town on a Saturday morning showed us that we would've liked to stay there for a week or so. It was a lovely, quaint country town, and the high school kids put on a tribal dancing show in the town square at noon, as they were all celebrating the 400th anniversary of Bartolomeu Dias' first stop at the most southern point of Africa. But naturally, the weather window opened up the next morning and we were off again, at last to round Cape Agulhas.

We had only a 260-mile run into Cape Town, and once we'd rounded the Cape, let the southwesterlies blow, for we would finally be going northwest and then we would need them. Not before then though, please.

We saw Cape Agulhas at 10 o'clock the next morning. How can I describe this sight? It was a gray, blustery day, spitting rain, cold and dreary, with rough waters bouncing TIGGER around. The wind was southeast, so it was behind us, and we were making good time on our trysail only. Out of the mist, I saw a low dark mound in the distance and knew that that was the Cape. We tried to stay about three miles offshore for safety, but we still wanted to be close enough to really see it. It is exactly as I thought it would be—the grayness, the rough waters and the mist. I was glad for a day like this. I didn't want a sunny day, pretty and calm, with blue water and a green coast. This day needed high drama. It was everything I had dreamed it would be, drawing from my imagination and all the stories I had read. No soft beauty here, it was all hardness and harshness, nature only allowing passage to those who deserved it and who worked for it. This is what Captain Cook saw on his first circumnavigation, most of his crew sick and dying from cholera; this is what Bartolomeu Dias saw when he went around the other way, several hundred years before Captain Cook, looking for a route to India.

We put our CD of bagpipe music on the player— to honor our Tartan 37—then we saluted the Cape and drank a toast to TIGGER who had taken us so far from home, to this desolate end of Africa. The bagpipes were as harsh and haunting as the Cape itself. We were both feeling pretty satisfied and more than a bit awestruck, knowing one more dream had been met. As the wind grabbed the sounds of the bagpipes playing *Amazing Grace*, and flung the notes across the waves towards the Cape, we both had tears in our eyes, and I knew this moment would become a memory that would thrill me forever.

Of course, the moments for high emotions are short moments on a boat, and life quickly got back to navigating and tending the sails. Things still looked good for a safe, easy ride into Cape Town. A southwesterly was coming, but that was now a good thing, right? Let it come!

Dave, however, had discovered a dreadful fact when he changed charts of the coastline. We'd run out of charts! The fellow who sold us the package of coastal charts had not included a detailed chart of about 60 miles after we rounded the Cape. And somehow, neither one of us had noticed. We had a large-scale chart. But without the detailed chart of this area, we would have to sail blind for the next 60 miles if we stayed close to the coast. Not keen on that idea, we moved eight miles offshore where we felt the chance of surprises was less. I let go of some anxiety when we pulled out the next detailed chart.

We had expected the weather to stay favorable all the way to Cape Town, but the afternoon weather report announced that gale-force east-southeast winds would be moving into our area in the evening. Sure enough, at 7 p.m. the wind suddenly started increasing. For so long we had feared winds out of the southwest, and now that we were around the Cape and would welcome them, our gale was out of the east-southeast! We battened down and prepared for a rough night. At least the wind was still behind us.

We were now in the clutches of the Benguela Current, which runs northwest along the west coast of South Africa.

With the current pushing us out away from land, and the wind behind us—by midnight it was up to 50 knots—we were having a hard time keeping a course back closer to the coast. For every mile we went seaward, the worse the angle to get into Cape Town. Rats!

The seas were also getting huge, rolling up behind us, lifting TIGGER and then rolling under her and on. As long as that was the way it went, we were fine, but every now and then, a wave would come from a slightly different angle and slam into the hull with a crash, sending lots of water into the cockpit and throwing us around. It was getting boring fast. Finally it wasn't just uncomfortable, it was a little dangerous, and the thing to do was to stop the boat. Around midnight, we hove-to on a starboard tack, at an angle that would slowly bring us toward the coast, just what we wanted. It's always easy to heave-to on TIGGER; just sheet that trysail in tight, turn the wheel hard to the wind, and tie it off. Perfect.

So we sat it out, wet and cold. I went below for an hour and when I came up to relieve Dave, he was very close to hypothermia. While I took extra pains to dress in foulweather jacket, pants, socks and boots, he had on his lightest jacket, no pants and he was barefoot! I helped him get down below, into dry clothes and wrapped up in some blankets. But then I had to get back up topsides, since we were close to the coast and lots of traffic. As it was I was breaking our rule; someone had to be topsides at all times.

Usually when we heave-to, the noise diminishes, and the motion of the boat is noticeably calmer. But nothing seemed to want to settle down that night, and it was noisy and rolly; not only because of the big waves, high winds and cold but because of the wind generator that we had installed in Durban. It did not have a brake and I wasn't about to tie the blades down to stop it in these conditions. Of course, the higher the wind, the noisier the generator. It would swing into the wind, scream piercingly as it caught the full force of the gale, and then swing off the wind with a heart stopping "Bang!" After that, all would be quiet for a few seconds, until the scenario was repeated. It was like having a jet engine in the cockpit. And this was the wind generator we'd bought because it was so quiet! Then a halyard loosened somewhere up forward and began banging on the mast. But I was not about to go forward to fix that problem either on such a night. So it banged, the wind generator screamed, the wind howled, and we slowly drifted closer to the coast.

Earlier, I had been talking on the VHF radio to several other boats that were also coming up the coast. Now I wanted to keep track of them. Since we were hove-to and the waves were so high, I would have a hard time seeing them until they were right upon us. They had all managed to stay close to shore, so were not getting the worst of the seas, though their winds were also 50 knots. Around 4 a.m., I was looking toward shore and saw a bright white masthead light, so I called one boat that I thought was near me, but got no answer. The light was white, not red or green, as we were accustomed to, but you sometimes see that outside the United States, and it warranted paying attention. Thoughts of all the collisions I had heard about during storms were running through my now worn-out brain, and I wondered who it was and whether they could see me. I called several times, and then made a general call for anyone in the vicinity of our position. No answer, but the light kept getting higher so I was sure it was approaching us. I was pretty anxious and was about to wake Dave when I looked carefully through the binoculars and saw it had no mast. What was going on? I finally tumbled to the fact that it was Jupiter, bright, intense Jupiter, getting higher in the sky, making it look like it was getting closer. It is especially brilliant there in the southern sky and it had scared what little wits I had left right out of me. I tried to have a nice laugh, but it was a little one for sure, as there wasn't much laughing that night.

At dawn, we were able to get moving again, and Dave had thawed out and was now bundled up properly in full foul-weather gear. We had moved farther in towards the coast, so our angle to Cape Town was a good one now. The wind had diminished to 35 knots, and the seas were better, not great, but better than they had been. We were only 20 miles from Table Bay, our entrance to Cape Town. We'd soon be tied up at the Royal Cape Yacht Club and more than ready for a good long rest. The Cape of Storms was behind us.

Then suddenly we went from 35 knots to no wind at all. And by the time we were five miles from Table Bay, it was dead calm, the seas were flat, and we were motoring. On the plus side, we saw dozens of seals lying on their backs on the surface, flippers raised in the air, so that they looked like dark brown logs with little branches. They were everywhere. Occasionally one would roll over, dive down and come up with a tasty morsel between its flippers. I know seals are not necessarily rare, but let's face it, seals are cute critters, obviously invented by Disney for our entertainment, and I was laughing as we motored by. They didn't even notice we were there.

All along the coast approaching Table Bay, we had a magnificent view of Table Mountain, the crowning glory of Cape Town, its protector and industrial-strength fan. The wind

Table Mountain and "tablecloth", Cape Town, South Africa

curves around the mountain and roars down across Cape Town, nestled at its base, then out across the coastal waters. The mountain has no peak—just a flat top, hence, the name *table*—and the clouds that form on top and drape down the sides of the mountain are called the table cloth. The day was dazzling gold with the sun shining on the green coastline and a white mist falling over the edge of the mountain, gilt-edged in the morning sun. It was so strange because there were no other clouds in the sky, just right there over the mountain. I had heard of it but could never quite picture in my mind how the clouds draped the mountain. Now I knew.

Dave was warm and rested now, and he fixed a cup of morning tea as we motored along the coast, enjoying the warmth of the sun and the beautiful panorama before us. We were laughing because we thought that after our rough and tumble night we would end up motoring into Cape Town and no one would believe the mess we'd been in the night before. But, as it turned out, we laughed a little too early. This was Cape Town after all, wasn't it? As we turned into the channel that led to the Royal Cape Yacht Club, the wind came roaring back, instantly at 30 knots on the nose. That made our maneuvering at close quarters to tie up to the dock interesting. Dave had to make two passes at the pier, with our friends who had arrived earlier standing ready to grab our lines and haul us in place since the wind wanted to blow us back out to the bay.

Soon we were greeting old friends, everyone talking at once, catching up on news and telling our stories. That is the way at cruising crossroads. There is almost always someone you know. And the famous Royal Cape Yacht Club was the place we wanted to safely tuck TIGGER while we enjoyed a short rest in Cape Town.

They say the wind always blows in Cape Town, and now I believe it. And it doesn't just blow—*It Blows*. One afternoon, it was clocked on a neighbor's boat at 70 knots. And the sun was shining! We had a spider web of lines from TIGGER to the finger pier, since we were the end boat on the dock and had no finger pier on the other side to stop us if we broke loose. I expressed my concern to the dockmaster one day, saying I was worried about the docks holding in such a heavy and sustained wind but he just replied, "Well, they've held this long, so I suppose they will hold long after you are gone." Somehow, I wasn't as comforted as I wished.

We were working in the cockpit when a South African sailboat backed out of its slip and rammed two American boats docked several slips away. It bounced off them and narrowly missed us while we were running up and down the dock, watching in horror. It then proceeded to bounce off a steel freighter that gave as good as it got. The last we saw of the boat and crew, there was a beer in the helmsman's hand and the whole bowsprit was hanging down the side, still held onto the boat by the lifelines. And they went out! They came back the next day, sober now (I think), with the bowsprit tied back in place by rope.

We were really looking forward to our next leg. I had read about the South Atlantic, and this run from Cape Town to Trinidad was supposedly a dream sail. No big storms to worry us; just steady trades and sunny days. That at least was the report. We planned to stop at St. Helena Island, 1,800 miles to the northwest, and from there go straight to Trinidad, another 3,700 miles. There was only one other possible stop, Ascension Island. But the British military ran the island, and we'd read that yachts were not welcome, so no stop there. Fortunately, we both enjoy long passages. This would be the longest yet.

But first, my brother, Bill, (who is younger than I am and who didn't throw snakes around my neck or entice me to throw mud pies) had friends who owned a vineyard in the wine country north of Cape Town, and they graciously invited us to stay with them at their farm for a day or two. South Africa has quite a thriving wine industry, and we stopped along the way at a cellar for a winetasting since our new friends only grew the grapes and didn't actually ferment them. I really liked one particular white wine and bought several bottles to savor on the long trip across the South Atlantic. I can report that it didn't last past Cape Town—Dave is not a tee-totaler like me. In Dave's world the sun is always over the yardarm. Our time at Shane-Anne and Evan's vineyard in the wine country of South Africa was a lovely interlude and another pleasant memory of that country.

The day before we were scheduled to leave for St. Helena, a friend noticed that the rudder for the wind steering unit looked bent but Dave said he was sure it was okay. And even though it did look a little crooked, with a small split at the very top of the rudder, the thought of wrestling it off, with TIG-GER in the water, in this crowded, windy and rocking marina, was too much for us. Like ostriches, we stuck our heads in the sand, hoping it would fix itself. We had put the rudder on with TIGGER in the water when we installed the unit in New Zealand and it was hell to get on; so no way were we going to do it.

28

Hello to Another Ocean

We said goodbye to South Africa by motoring out of Table Bay in a calm—a very rare occasion. It took 14 days to sail to St. Helena on mostly southeast winds; up and down, rough and calm, but nothing dramatic for a change. On a rhumbline, the wind was right behind us. We wandered a bit, trying to keep the wind off to the side, so the rolling wouldn't be so bad. But in my log, I mentioned that we were back to the rhythm of the seas, days of reading, napping and wondering what to have to eat! Some days, I would bake bread or cookies. Dave would cook the meals.

In our first few days out, we saw lots of seals languishing on the surface, some penguins, and once a sunfish swam by, a weird looking fish as it seemed to be all head! I just happened to glance over the side, and there it was, large and round. It was the only time I ever saw one. A very prehistoric looking creature.

Since the wind stayed from the southeast, we didn't have to mess with the sails much. But, if we did, it was guaranteed to be at 3 a.m. on my off-watch. I would hear, "Honey, would you help me, I think we should jibe," and I'd have to get up to help with what in my opinion was the totally unnecessary middle-of-the-night jibe. One night, just as I was getting back to sleep, a net bag above my head broke open and a dozen oranges fell on my head. Then I was really grumpy.

Midway through this leg the reacher-drifter finally gave up the ghost after 20 years of hard service. It was up in light air and just ripped from luff to leach in the middle of the lower section.

Arriving in James Bay in St. Helena, we first tried to anchor in 52 feet of water. Dave and I had our usual spirited discussion about his wanting to be in the shallowest water possible because he had to crank the anchor back up, and I wanted to be as far away from other boats as possible so we didn't have to worry about a wind shift and hitting someone. We immediately swung too close to another boat and he had to crank the anchor back up, so we could move into 72 feet of water. As I was motoring around looking for a good spot, the engine overheated, and I heard a pop as smoke started billowing out of the engine compartment. "No, wait, it's steam, not smoke," I yelled to Dave as I shut down the engine. A blown hose that Dave put back, and we got to our anchoring spot and stopped—blessed silence and stillness. Then I heard a funny beeping and looked at the instruments. The knotmeter had died. Oh well, no place to sail to tonight, tomorrow's another day to fix it all.

I have always thought of St. Helena as the place where Napoleon was exiled after his defeat. Although that is its claim to fame, it's also a nifty little island all on its own. Rising right out of the ocean to steep mountains, it's all rock and crashing waves on the shoreline. After a wild and winding ride to the top of the mountains on one of the few roads, you will find verdant farm fields. The mountains are eroded at the top and that's where the farming is done; lots of it and green, green, green.

Jamestown is nestled in a long, narrow valley between two cliffs, rising as the valley rises with the hills. It is a small town, with the feel of an eighteenth century English village. Since

Jamestown, St. Helena, South Atlantic

the only way to get to St. Helena is by boat, the mail and supplies come just once a month. Not many tourists visit, except
those of us who come by our own yachts. Everyone had to
climb the 699 steps from the base of the town to get to the
community at the top of one cliff. Everyone but me. I was told
that at one time the only school was on top, and the children
from down below had to climb the stairs each day to go to
school. Then after school, they would straddle the banisters
and slide down the cliff face.

We also spent a day touring the island in a 1928 touring car,
rebuilt a time or two no doubt. It was a convertible, with pro-
gressively raised seats toward the back to give a good view to
everyone. We sat in the back, and I felt like Granny Clampett.
Narrow winding roads pointed straight to the sky when they
weren't bending back on themselves. I had to close my eyes
once or twice, but what a spectacular view when I opened them!

Napoleon's grave is in a quiet little glade, overrun by flowers and incredibly beautiful and peaceful. Only he's not there
anymore. The French wanted him back, and he was carted off

to France many years ago. So, even though he chose it as his place to rest for eternity, the grave is empty.

St. Helena does not have a quiet harbor in which to anchor. Instead, it is an open roadstead, with waves rolling in from other continents and crashing on its shores. The Jamestown anchorage is on the west side of the island, at least protected from the southeast trades, but still rolling and uncomfortable. In order to get into the jetty, the town runs a shuttle, a longboat that comes through the anchorage to pick you up and then ferry you to the jetty. Once there, as a swell raises the longboat level with the dock, you jump off before the swell takes the boat back down; sort of like an elevator. There was a rope suspended out over the water to grab just in case you were on the up when the boat was on the down. It was all very exciting, and there always seemed to be an audience to observe any acrobatics.

One day, seven of us took the longboat to go back to our yachts. We got out into the anchorage, and the motor died. The driver was trying to get it started, but it was an ebb tide

Farmer hauling hay, St. Helena, South Atlantic

and we were drifting out to sea. We drifted passed Dennis and Kathryn on FLAMBOYANT, a red ferrocement boat from New Zealand. Dennis saw what had happened, jumped into his dinghy and rowed after us with a line. As we passed Mike on POTLATCH, a cruising catamaran from Hawaii, Dennis still hadn't caught us. So Mike took the other end of the line from Dennis and tied more line to it, since what Dennis had was too short by that time, and he kept tying lines until Dennis was able to reach us, and we got the rope secured to the longboat. Then Mike hauled on the line and pulled us back to POT-LATCH, just like reeling in a fish! After they tied us to the cata-maran, Mike's wife, Candace, served us dried tuna and cool water while the driver worked on the engine (with four other men giving suggestions). Finally, the driver, in spite of all the suggestions, got the engine going, and we thanked FLAMBOY-ANT for the rescue, and POTLATCH for their hospitality, and were on our way.

After that it was time to set out on the 3,700-mile leg straight to Trinidad where we expected steady southeasterlies. The log records that the days were sunny and the winds steady from the southeast just as we'd hoped. In fact, there are quite a few entries reading "conditions same" in the first five days. I always seemed to experience some depression and loneliness the first days at sea, but this time it was different; it was crush-ing and painful, maybe because we faced a 30-day passage, the longest ever. I never gave a thought to the possibility that it was a premonition of bad things to come. Dave, ever desirous to make me happy, suggested that we stop at Ascension Island. Even though we might not be welcome, perhaps they would let us stay a day or so. Perhaps the sight of people and land would cheer me up. With that reward ahead of us, I was able to read, putter and watch the waves in emotional comfort.

We were seeing lots of seabirds again—frigates, gannets, tropicbirds, boobies, and a petrel. Fish were jumping all around. In fact, we would travel through patches of ocean where, for miles around us, there would be fish. I also saw something I hadn't seen before. A flying fish would leave the water and soar over the waves, just like always. But this time, right behind him, a dorado would skim through the water close to the surface, racing after it, as if the dorado knew where the flying fish was going to land. Several times, I saw schools of some kind of silver fish, not ballyhoo or small bait fish, but big fish, like tuna, surfing in the following seas, thousands of them. The water was clean and clear and that deep, open-ocean blue that can mesmerize and hypnotize with its indescribable shade. Oh, if this is the way it will be to Trinidad, it will be perfect.

On the fifth day out, Dave looked at the wind steering and told me the crack looked a little bigger, the rudder looked a little more bent, and he sure hoped it would last until Ascension Island where he could work on it. Five minutes later we heard a thud and ran to the stern. The rudder was gone, sunk to 20,000 feet in the indescribable blue. Willy was now just half a helmsman, and we still had over 3,000 miles to Trinidad. It was no longer a matter of fixing it, now it had to be replaced. I hand-steered while Dave hooked up our sick autopilot and got it to work until the middle of the night when it gave up, and then he steered until morning.

We were still more than 200 miles from Ascension, so Dave babied the autopilot on his watch. He has infinite patience with things mechanical and electrical. Even when they die, he thinks he can bring them back to life. I don't know if he has ever said, "It's dead. I can't fix it," except when the autopilot motor fried in Australia and was nothing but stinky smoke and charred plastic. I, on the other hand, do not have that kind of patience, so on my watches I would baby the autopilot for 30 minutes and then hand-steer for an hour or so before giving it another try.

For sailors who have never done long passages, hand steering doesn't sound so hard, but it is actually very fatiguing, physically and mentally—and knowing we had thousands of miles to go without our wind steering system was a killer. In our whole trip, we had hand steered maybe 15 hours, not counting going in and out of ports. We had heard from a friend on the net that they were sure we could get a new rudder built in Ascension, so I held on to that thought for comfort. Fortunately the weather was still ideal, southeast trades at 15–20 knots, moderate seas and sunny skies.

Still there was the nagging feeling that our luck was running low. TIGGER was tired and old, and so were we. We had all come almost 30,000 miles, and though we took good care of TIGGER, it almost felt like her spirit was weary. None of the instruments worked except for the depthsounder, the solar panels had quit putting out power, the reacher-drifter was unusable and now the wind steering was shot. What could happen next? I tried not to think about it.

We arrived at Ascension in the dark. For a couple who never entered an unfamiliar harbor at night, we were certainly becoming risk takers, but the anchorage there is wide open, and the surrounding waters deep, so we motored along the coast in the overcast darkness. I called Ascension Radio and they referred us to an oil tanker that was anchored out to help us orient ourselves to the anchorage. The tanker told us to go to the north side of them and then head straight toward shore. "No obstacles," they said, "well, except for the unlit mooring buoy. Oh, and there's also a floating hose." Great. But just as we turned toward the shoreline, the clouds parted on a half moon, and there was light to see both the obstacles. We anchored in 45 feet of water near a group of fishing boats. Damn, too close, and we had to move as usual. Then, settled at last, we enjoyed an uninterrupted night's sleep.

In the dark, Ascension Island had looked like a scene from an old James Bond movie, and in the daylight it still looked the same. It's just a barren rock in the middle of the ocean, its hillsides studded with communications equipment. From the anchorage, it looked like a huge pile of volcanic rubble, although someone told us later that there was a green area back in the hills. In the morning sunshine, we could see that the water under the boat was crystal clear, and

there were about a hundred small triggerfish lounging in
TIGGER's shade.

Ascension presents the same challenge as St. Helena, in
that there's no real harbor to speak of, and though we were on
the west side of the island, protected from the southeast winds,
it was quite rolly. Again, the pier is a narrow shelf cut into the
rock on the face of a low cliff with the requisite line hanging
over the dock if you missed your step. There's no longboat here
to pick you up, and when you bring your own dinghy in, it is
the same as St. Helena, and you have to ride the swell up and
jump out before the swell passes and the dinghy descends. Ascension also has a beach, but it is very steep and to land a
dinghy there requires that you ride the surf in, jump out and
haul the dinghy and yourselves up above the waterline quickly,
before the retreating wave hauls you back out again. Some
days were worse than others. The beach was primarily sand,
but did have rocks scattered along the water's edge to give you
a good scare.

After checking in, our mission was to find someone who
could fabricate a replacement rudder, and we soon found an
American machinist, who said, " No problem, I can make it in
several hours." We gave him the dimensions, or what we
thought the dimensions were, since we had no drawings and
the only pattern was the rudder itself, at the bottom of the
ocean. His several hours turned to four days, but he delivered
us a rudder, made of aircraft aluminum and heavy as can be.
We thanked him and asked him for the charges. He told us not
to worry and that it was on Uncle Sam.

While we waited, we explored the island within walking
distance. We were too worried about the rudder to really be curious, but I do remember that the little store serving the civil-
ians working on the island had more chocolates than I had
ever seen in a store its size. My kind of store! Then there was
a little restaurant that served mashed peas as a side dish. They
looked at me when I said this must be a British thing.

"Don't you have mashed peas in America?" the girl behind

the counter asked, which got me thinking about back when I used to mash my peas as a kid. I have some English heritage, so I guess my childhood habit came from that.

We decided to try a beach landing after I had been left dangling—literally—at the dock on our previous landing attempt. I had grabbed the rope as the swell brought us up but didn't jump fast enough. The swell went down and so did the dinghy. And I was stuck holding the rope, hanging on for dear life, hanging above the water until the dinghy came zooming back up on the next swell, which I then used to launch myself onto the dock. A beach landing had to be easier than that.

We rode the surf in and got the dinghy quickly out of harm's way. It was laundry day, so I hauled two plastic bags full of clothes over to the water faucet by one of the buildings where I asked permission to use the water from a person watching me. He smiled and nodded, so I went about washing the laundry at the side of a military building. Then, after doing the laundry, and putting it in a plastic bag to bring back to the boat to dry, we had to get back through the surf. We got the dinghy to the water's edge and Dave pushed it out and jumped in just as the wave started going out. I jumped, but too late, and the dinghy swept by me. I grabbed it and was dragged out with the wave, in water up to my neck. The wave brought the dinghy (and me) back into shore, and I managed to climb in and start rowing like crazy to avoid the rocks while Dave was trying to start the outboard. Whew! My freshly washed clothes remained salt water free, however, even if I didn't. We figured our landing luck was running out, and I was really glad when the rudder came the next day.

It looked good, but it was too big; our fault, we just didn't remember how narrow the old one was. So Dave spent an afternoon sawing it down to the right size with a handsaw, which was very tedious with aluminum filings flying everywhere. Finally we got it back on and we were ready to go. But we still had to check out and by the time that was done the next day, we were both too tired from the trips to shore to go anywhere, so we decided we needed one last long night's sleep. We did so quite peacefully now that we had the rudder.

Even with its rough landings, Ascension was a unique and interesting place, sort of like a science station on the moon. I asked one of the Americans if all they did was monitor communications. He'd told us that they'd know within 30 seconds if a missile had been launched anywhere in the world. Sixty seconds later they'd know who had done it and where it was headed. Did they also star watch? He said they do monitor deep space, and I had a Carl Sagan moment—space probes and all that. It seems much more interesting and positive than missile watching.

The island hadn't even faded completely from view when the new rudder snapped and fell off, just like the old one. This time the side pressure bent it like a twig, and it was gone in several hours. My God, what a disappointment. When I heard the crack, and then the thump, I went numb. I knew what it was and what it meant, even though my mind didn't want to face reality. All that bloody work to take the old post off and put the new one on and here we were back to hand steering with 3,000 miles to Trinidad. I said, "Well, we can do it, we have no choice, people hand steered before, you do what you have to do, at least we have our main rudder." Blah, blah, blah. I really was numb.

Later in the day, when the numbness began wearing off, my beginning passage depression was worse than ever. I felt like someone had died. I had never been really frightened in the whole trip, at least not like this. I had been anxious, worried and nervous many times. But I felt more frightened and alone over this problem than any storm or breakdown we had encountered. The freedom was gone, we were tied to the wheel. I couldn't stretch anymore. I'd had terrible dreams ever since the original rudder fell off, and that night they were worse than ever. I woke up sad and disoriented.

Okay, enough of feeling sorry for myself. How could we

create a new self-steering mechanism for TIGGER? The morning weather was perfect, the seas were gentle, and the winds
were the usual steady southeast 15–20 knots. For that I was
thankful. We turned our attention to trying to solve this problem. First, the autopilot. Dave worked for several hours with
the wheel off, and the autopilot in pieces, investigating the
possibility that he could fix it. I steered with the emergency
tiller. Actually, that was good practice. I hadn't used it before.
It's amazing how much more you can feel the rudder with the
tiller than with the wheel. I had heard that before, now I had
the experience.

Dave decided the autopilot was finally dead for good. So it
was on to something else. As I was steering with the emergency tiller, I commented that it was too bad we couldn't rig
up something to steer with this tiller, not the wheel. Then
Dave took the idea a bit farther and wondered if he couldn't
maybe rig up a line from the wind steering unit to the wheel.

In fact, the idea was in no way out of the ordinary. Many
wind steering units are designed without their own rudder and
control a vessel in just this way. Dave worked several hours rig-
ging lines this way and that until he finally got it working and
TIGGER was steering herself, if somewhat erratically. The system wasn't perfect. There were chafe spots on the lines that
couldn't be protected. But it was still very heartening.

After that Dave decided to try to figure a way to attach our
little tiller steering unit to the wheel. That is, treat the wheel
as a tiller. He set about mounting a small platform on the side
of the cockpit in line with the wheel. Then he mounted the
tiller steering unit, with its moving arm secured to a spoke in
the wheel. When the course needed changing, the tiller arm
retracted or extended, moving the spoke clockwise or coun-
terclockwise, thus turning the whole wheel. Revolutionary!
We had an autopilot! The whole world looked better, brighter,
safer and free again. We'd spent well over $2,000 on the two
autopilots we bought before we left the United States. We'd
spent about $1,500 more repairing them in various ports. But

in the end it was this jury-rigged system that steered us to Trinidad.

Finally I could relax again, and our days returned to their usual passage schedule: on-watch reading, puttering in the cockpit, or in my case staring at the sea and dreaming; off-watch napping, reading, listening to the radio or fishing. Life was good, the winds stayed a steady southeasterly and the sails only occasionally needed adjusting. I heard on the radio that there was a partial solar eclipse, but we were too far south so the sun shone brightly all day long.

I was on watch when the engine quit. I was running it to charge the batteries when I heard a clunk and then a horrible grinding. I knew it was the engine, but not what was wrong, so I put it in neutral and shut it down. Dave came topsides immediately, and I told him what I had done. He tried to start it, but no dice. He stuck his head in the engine compartment and fiddled with this and checked that. We tried again, and in a hushed voice, he said, "The flywheel's not turning, it's gone."

Jury-rigged autopilot, South Atlantic

"Okay," I said, "Wind-steering unit inoperable, engine inoperable, but we still have TIGGER, she is sound and the wind is blowing, and we have solar panels and a wind generator to charge batteries."

"Well," Dave replied, "Don't forget, the solar panels are not putting power into the batteries, I guess they have a broken wire somewhere or the cells are dead."

"Okay, but we still have TIGGER and the wind generator."

"Well," Dave replied again, "actually, the wind generator does not come anywhere close to supplying us with the power we need to run the refrigeration and navigation lights and watermaker and radio."

Damn, damn, damn.

"Okay, we turn off the refrigerator, we don't need to worry about water, as we will be getting rain when we get to the doldrums, and we can leave the lights off at night until we see a ship, and then turn them on. We are always on watch, so we don't have to depend on their missing us by seeing our nav lights." I didn't cry because this latest debacle held only inconvenience, not terror for me. Still it did leave a little nagging anxiety, because things were breaking down at an increasing rate and I wondered what would be next? Banish that thought, I told myself, and get busy turning off the refrigerator, deciding what few radio contacts we want to continue and get back to enjoying this fabulous sail. We were, after all, on a sailboat. I was going to miss the cold drinks, but I could rough it. Dave would not miss cold drinks. Like Europeans he prefers his drinks, including beer, room temperature. Yuk!

More days went by in this lovely ocean that was treating us so well weatherwise. I attribute fate and a weary TIGGER to the demise of some of our equipment. The South Atlantic was being as gentle as possible with us.

Dave was talking on the radio one day to our friends on KULLA II, the Swedish boat, and they recommended we go to Brazil to effect engine repairs. When Dave told him we didn't have a visa, Gunnar said he had been able to get a visa upon arrival. When Dave said, "Yes, but Americans need a prior visa," Gunnar said, "Oh, no, I know other Americans who didn't have one," and Dave and I looked at each other. Was the cruising guide wrong? Had they changed the rules? It would be nice to have TIGGER fixed up before we had to face the upcoming, mostly windless doldrums, near the equator. So, after another radio conference with Jim and Meredith on ODYSSEY, Americans who also had no prior visa, we decided that if Brazil would take us, all four of us would stop and request emergency permission to stay and get the engine fixed. Jim and Meredith would tow us into the harbor if need be. After all, that is the rule of the sea, isn't it? Countries grant safe haven to those in trouble.

29

&

Take Us In, Brazil—Please

First we changed course for Fernando de Noronha, a small island off the coast of central Brazil, then to Fortaleza, a large port city, with easy access for an engineless sailboat. Maybe we'd be motoring through the doldrums, sipping cold drinks after all!

A short stop in Fernando de Noronha highlighted a forgotten fact: that Brazilians speak Portuguese, not Spanish. Not that we speak Spanish, but we had managed to communicate in Spanish speaking countries. Portuguese was another story.

The run from Fernando de Noronha to Fortaleza was 360 miles almost due west. And with the brisk west-setting current, and the lovely south wind, we zipped along on a beam reach, making record time to our engine repair. Or so we thought.

The little snag in our plan was that we didn't have detailed charts of the coast. In fact, our smallest-scale chart was the entire South Atlantic Ocean. Gunnar, however, had given us GPS waypoints, and we could see on our chart that there were no islands or significant rocks in our way. But the sea bottom shelves far from shore on this part of the coast and we saw 100-foot depths long before we saw land.

I had developed a pretty good "chart to visual land" perception in the preceding miles of our journey, but I didn't have
a good "GPS waypoint to visual land" perception. When we
got to the waypoint, I couldn't figure out where we were in re-
lation to what Gunnar told us to expect to see. So we sailed in
circles for several hours until ODYSSEY came sailing up behind
us and showed us the way. I guess they had a better sense of
perception than I did, because they sailed right up the coast,
around the corner, and then headed for the hotel and marina!
We followed, but carefully. It is quite nerve-wracking to navi-
gate without charts, if you can even call that navigating.

Our time in Fortaleza was short and not so sweet. We
found people who spoke English, but the immigration officer
was not one of them. When the dockmaster took Dave and
Jim to Customs and Immigration to check in, the officer asked
for visas. When the dockmaster, Jorge, told him in Portuguese
that we had none, that we were requesting an emergency visa
due to engine failure and need for repairs, the officer started
shouting in Portuguese. He told them, "How dare you come
without a visa, get back to the boat and do not leave the
grounds." (This was translated by Jorge). Then he told them to
come back tomorrow, since he didn't have time for them
today. I guess, "go away," was repeated several times.

Back to the boat they came, and to get things rolling,
Dave went looking for someone to fix the engine. Dave had
not fully examined it and wasn't sure what was wrong, but
when a fellow who spoke good English came by the boat to
look, he told him he would have to take the engine out. Then
the complications began. They would have to bring a hoist,
find a way to get it on the dock next to TIGGER and then find
a way to transport the engine to his shop. The good news was
that he was sure he could fix it, although he admitted that the
parts might be hard to find.

Meredith and Jim, being the young, free spirits they were,
decided to explore the town and do something fun as long as
they were there. But Dave and I, being older and more con-

servative, elected to do as the immigration officer ordered and
stay put. Maybe the free spirits never get caught, but I was held
at gunpoint in a Turkish airport many years ago, an experience
that sort of stuck with me. I have a healthy respect for the
petty bureaucrat who wields a heavy stick, especially when the
sticks are loaded.

Four days later, after much fussing and talking, the engine
repair fellow said it would be many weeks before the parts
would get there to fix the engine. And we learned that if we
wanted an emergency visa, it would cost about $2,500 in legal
fees for a 15-day stay. After that bit of news, Meredith stopped
by terribly upset. She had gotten into a heated exchange with
a German yachtsman who'd yelled at her that Americans were
arrogant. I'm not sure what the basis of his accusation was, but
the lack of a visa might have had something to do with it. Finally Jorge the dockmaster said he could not help us anymore
with anything. Dave and I decided that sailing to Trinidad
without an engine might not be such a bad idea after all. Cold
drinks aren't everything. Keeping our necks and skin intact,
and TIGGER in our possession was.

The next afternoon, ODYSSEY towed us out of the harbor
and we set sail on a northwest course to reach the 100-fathom
line and find the north-setting French Equatorial Current, in
order to press on to Trinidad. The wind was southeast and the
seas flat. The country may not have been friendly, but the
coast was lovely. I was happy and free again. We only had
1,600 miles to Trinidad, and we had a fair wind and current to
take us. TIGGER was sound and we had good sails. We were fine.

We crossed the equator on the third day around sunset.
TIGGER was back in the Northern Hemisphere for the first time
in three and a half years, and we drank a toast to the Northern
Hemisphere and all the good things in it—home and family—
then saluted King Neptune with a drop or two.

It was on this leg that we broke our daily record, sailing
196 miles in 24 hours. The current was carrying us at an as-
tounding pace, and the winds were mostly steady and still out

of the southeast, so we were moving along smartly. It was beastly hot near the equator, but we could be naked again, thank goodness, although every now and then, a squall would come across, dump buckets of cold water on us before moving on. These squalls would come up quite suddenly, and we had to be especially careful because of our jury-rigged steering system. If a gust knocked TIGGER dramatically off course, the tiller pilot would try to correct but get stuck at the end of the stroke. Then the sails would backwind, and all hell would break loose. Ultimately we'd have to undo the lashings to the wheel in order to get back on course, and set the system back up again. This may sound easy, but it was actually very difficult, especially in gusty conditions, with the sails flapping like crazy. When we got through the doldrums, things settled down, and the tiller pilot could handle the small course changes easily again.

Most of the squally weather was off the mouth of the Amazon River. We never actually saw this great river, but there was plenty of evidence of its existence when the water turned muddy brown, the seas became rough and the squalls came more often. We were still concerned about the doldrums—I had visions of us just sitting there slowly drifting until we ran out of drinking water. But our windless spell only lasted about four hours, after which the wind picked up, the skies dumped another ton of water on us, and we were once again under way.

Alas, but the fickle finger of fate was not yet done with us. On the seventh day out, the jib roller-furling seized up, with the sail out. The ball bearings just spilled out over the deck and that was that. Dave managed to hand turn the drum, and we rolled in the sail. But here we were again, our list of things to fix in Trinidad was seemingly getting longer with every passing day, and we were reduced to sailing with only the main. Poor TIGGER was losing systems right and left.

At 6 o'clock in the morning of the 11th day, we rounded the northeast corner of the island of Trinidad. Ha! We'd made it! We only had to sail along the northern coast, a mere 25 miles, then cut through the Boca de Monos (Monos Channel) to the anchorage in Chaguaramas Bay, on the northwest side of the island. That is where yachts check in and where the marinas and repair facilities are located. We had been averaging about 6 to 7 knots for the past 11 days, so we were taking our speed for granted. We would be there by noon.

As it turned out, however, we had one more adventure to stumble through before we could rest, both TIGGER and her crew. When we turned the corner and pointed west, it was like the wind machine got turned off. The island shadowed the southeast wind, and it went from 20 knots to 3 knots in about 15 minutes. If there was ever a doldrums for us, this was it. As the day wore on, we first tried the torn reacher-drifter, which I'd repaired with duct tape—proper sail repair tape was used up many miles ago. But it lasted only about 30 minutes before the tape broke loose and the sail tore even more.

Then we tried the spinnaker. But it also had a small rip, and when a 10-knot puff made it even bigger, that sail came down as well. Whew! We had a heavy mainsail, a heavy storm trysail and a heavy storm staysail—and no wind. We didn't have to be anchored that night. We could have taken the larger, more open Boca del Dragon and stood off the island until morning. But we wanted to be anchored. By God, we were getting to that anchorage that night. We were going to sleep with the anchor down!

So we tiptoed along the coast, mostly drifting with the west-setting current, and each time the wind puffed a little, we joyously raised the main to catch it. As the puff disappeared, we swore and lowered the main and drifted along a bit more.

Dave is an ex-racer. He knows wind and sail angle, and they are close to his heart. But I heard a lot of swearing that day as he worked the few sails we had left, trying to inch TIGGER along the coast and around the corner toward our anchorage.

At one point, I turned around and saw an interisland ferry coming up behind us. We were only about 50 yards off the shore as we were trying to stay as close as possible to cut down on our distance, and there was plenty of water beneath our keel. I called the ferry to tell the captain we were engineless and couldn't maneuver. He didn't answer but kept coming on a course that would run right over us. I called again. He didn't answer. Come on, answer the radio! We had no place to go to get out of his way, and no way to get there. When I began thinking about grabbing the ship's papers and taking a dive, Dave called him and he answered, "No problem, mon. We miss you." And he did, but not by much.

The Boca de Monos is a narrow channel between the main island of Trinidad and a small island off the north coast. The sides of both landmasses are steep cliffs in most places with a few beaches and jungle. The channel is only a mile and a half long, and we expected a bit of wind would be funneling through it, so we entered the channel at 4 p.m. with high expectations. The wind momentarily came up to keep us off the big rock in the middle of the entrance, but then shifted to the north, behind us and fell light, very light. Dave adjusted the main while I put up the storm staysail. The plan called for jibing down the channel to make our way against the current, but we didn't have much room to work, so they were very short jibes. Our forward speed varied from half a knot to 1.5 knots, and I was scrambling every few minutes as Dave yelled, "Jibe!" He was so good with this pitiful wind. He would steer as close to shore on one side as he could get, then we would jibe. Then off to the other side as close to shore as we could get and jibe again. There was little room to really sail, but we were making forward progress, slowly, very slowly. I watched the shadows get longer and longer as the sun fell behind the cliffs on the west side of the channel. Then the blue sky got milky as the sun began its slide into the west.

About halfway through, a fisherman came roaring by in a fishing skiff with a nice powerful outboard. I hailed him as our savior and asked if he would tow us toward Chaguaramas Bay, which was now less than three miles away. I said we would give him $10 to tow us to the end of the channel, a half-mile. He just looked at us. "Okay," I said, "$20," thinking that ought to clinch it. He looked at me solemnly and said, "I do it for $200, $200 U.S."

I kept a straight face, and said, "No, but thanks for stopping."

He nodded and replied, "I must go fishing, you know."

So on we tiptoed.

It was dark when we rounded the end of the channel and wound our way to the anchorage. If a chart could be worn down by eyes studying it, boring into it, memorizing it, that chart would be shredded. I felt if I looked at it often enough, the channel would get wider, the water deeper and the winds heavier.

We did find some wind as we came around, though it was right on the nose. It wasn't much, but with the storm staysail and full main up, the 8 knots of breeze at least gave us some forward movement. Now we were tacking instead of jibing. We had one little island to miss, and it was inky black with no moon. If there were boats anchored somewhere, we couldn't see them. There were harsh lights on shore, security lights of some kind, but they only blinded us to what was around us. I got up on the bow with a spotlight and shined it first on the mainland, then as we got very close, I ran back and we tacked. Then I ran to the bow and shined the spotlight on the little island we had to miss, after which I ran back and we tacked the other way. We had so little distance to go, but still no anchor lights. Where was everyone? The water was 30 feet deep, so we could throw a hook down right here if we had to, but the guidebook said this was a channel for small ships. We finally cleared the island, and the bay opened up. Ahead, there was a lone sailboat anchor light and the lights of a small ship. We headed for that spot. If they were anchored, we could anchor.

We hauled down sails near the sailboat, dropped the hook and were in Trinidad. Wow! We'd sailed 5,556 miles from Cape Town, across the best ocean in the world. Maybe it wasn't all good luck, but certainly it was the best sailing we'd experienced in our long journey. And now it was time for a rest. Good night Dave, good night TIGGER. Good night Trinidad!

The next morning, we woke up, stuck our heads out the companionway, and holy cow, there were a thousand boats in front of us. Some were at anchor, but most were on the hard at the numerous haulout and repair facilities that line Chaguaramas Bay. Since it is a designated anchorage, apparently no one had anchor lights on the night before.

The time in Trinidad was a busy one, what with all the things that needed to be fixed: no sightseeing, no relaxing on the beach, no snorkeling, no side trips to quiet coves. We fixed the boat and moved on. We were headed home. It was now late May, and it was important to get settled before hurricane season started. So while in Trinidad, we took a slip at the Crew's Nest Marina and spent our days finding people to fix things. Since the Chaguaramas Bay area has been transformed into a cruisers' maintenance heaven, everything we needed was right there. The work was good, and the prices were reasonable; not cheap, but reasonable.

While we waited for a new wind steering rudder to be sent from Germany, Dave lifted the transmission from the engine block and took the transmission to a mechanic who had it up and running in two days. He also got the bearings for the roller furling for us. In no time, Dave had the transmission and the roller furling back in order.

It turned out the engine problem hadn't really been an engine problem after all. When we couldn't get the engine fixed in Brazil, Jim from ODYSSEY and Dave had tried to take the transmission off to look at it. But after hanging upside down in the cockpit locker trying to remove what they'd thought were the bolts holding it to the engine, they had concluded that the transmission housing was somehow permanently attached; that's why the repairman in Brazil had thought he would have to pull the engine. When we got to Trinidad, however, we found that, without the bolts holding it in place, just the motion of the boat had knocked the transmission loose from the engine block. All Dave had to do was pick it up and carry it to the repair shop. The engine was fine. It was the transmission that had seized up.

30

⟨∽⟩

The Circle Closes

In less than three weeks, we were ready to shove off and get on to completing the circle. We still had a little over 2,000 miles to go. But we planned to do it with only one stop: 1,200 miles to the Cayman Islands, a stop for fresh foods, then another 900 right into Galveston Bay.

The winds were fair, and the west-setting current gave us a boost the first 36 hours or so, but I had my usual depression those first two days. I felt so split. It was as if two voices were carrying on a debate in my head in those early days offshore. One side would cry, "Go back, go back, it's safe back there, tied to the dock. There are lights, and people, and safety." But another part would shout, "Go on, go on, out there is freedom. There is the sea and the sky and adventure. Just you and Dave and TIGGER. Go on."

All my life, I have needed to know what is just over the horizon. Have you ever noticed how the sun reflects off the back side of the clouds after it goes down? How it makes those golden rays streaming from a fire that you can't see? I have always had a need to see where those rays were coming from. Those golden rays have led my wanderings all these years. It feels like an emptiness that would be filled if I was just "over there." The hours of sunset and twilight are melancholy hours for me, bringing on some yearning I can't define, even to myself. It's a pull. The western horizon just makes me itch to go that way.

We caught a mooring in the harbor in front of George Town at Grand Cayman Island. It was late evening, already dark. Our night entrances were becoming routine. It had been an 8-day, 12-hour, 1,267-mile run. That was about 149 miles per day, a very good speed for TIGGER. And though we have gone faster, all systems were working and it was a most pleasant trip. We figured two days maximum here, and then the final miles home.

As we got closer to the end of our journey, I spent more and more time looking at the sea and wondering about our future. It will be hard to see the journey end, I realized. What will happen next? Where will we go that is bigger and better than where we have been? I would counter those feelings and thoughts with daydreams of time with my children, laughing with my grandsons, hugging them. How I longed to put my arms around their sturdy little bodies and feel them hug me back. Maternal urges run deep, and I hadn't lost mine. There is nothing so beautiful in this world as the smell and feel of a little child, soft and sweet. I still had a chance to bond with them, before they were at the age when the experience of growing up—and the world—could distance us. I had plans for those boys!

I knew my children didn't need me anymore. Perhaps because I was a single parent, we'd been tied tight to each other, and they'd depended on me long after other children were gone and on their own. But four and a half years had cut that tie, and now they were strong, truly independent adults. I saw the change each time I went home for a visit. It was both painful and joyful to see them this way. Now we were equals.

What gave me the most comfort was the knowledge that I had Dave as my partner now. We were a team, both in our sailing and in our marriage. I knew I could never again be that cynical, solitary woman I once was. With Dave I had become an open and free heart. I loved him for that gift to me. So the journey, this journey, was almost over, but our marriage and our life together had really just started.

The two days in the Caymans were wet. It rained torrentially most of both days, with only a few hours respite. So we did our errands in the rain and really didn't mind. The nice thing about wearing shorts and T-shirts as a uniform is that no one cares if they get wet. The air was warm, the rain was warm, the puddles were warm and I didn't have a corporate meeting to go to.

We did see enough to think we might like to visit again some day, since the Caymans are one of those places where visitors clearly are welcome. I like to smile at people and have them smile back. That is not always the case in other parts of the world, just as it is not always the case in the United States. But they did smile in the Caymans, and everyone was pleasant without acting obsequious. Several cruise ships came in and dumped hundreds of people in front of the duty-free shops, and the little town would be crowded and noisy. Then two hours later, they would all get back on the cruise ship, and the town would slow down again. I wonder what the locals thought of us. We didn't spend money like the cruise ship people did. But we happily splashed through the puddles and laughed as the rain dripped off our noses.

The wind and seas were quiet as we left Grand Cayman and started our last 980-mile run. We would pick up the north-setting current as we went through the Yucatán Channel, and hopefully it would give us a nice little boost home. The rain stopped when we left Grand Cayman, and the weather stayed settled right up to the first stop at the Galveston Yacht Club.

I had one last major fright the second night out. I was on watch in the cockpit with my little red-lens reading light—red lens because I didn't want to ruin my night vision with a regular light—when a movement caught my eye. I looked up and saw a big freighter passing us about 200 yards to starboard. It was going the other way so it'd been coming toward us. How did I ever miss seeing it coming? It was very dark so its lights would have been visible for a long way. Even if it were coming exactly on our bow where it would be the least visible, it was still lit up with working lights I should have seen. How could this happen? I thought I'd learned my lesson way back in the Pacific. God only knows why the freighter missed us, and we are not fish food with the kids wondering what happened to us. I am not irresponsible. I don't spend time down below. I stay in the cockpit, and I look around every 10 minutes. I was disgusted with myself.

The next day, I saw three whales slowly swim by about 50 yards off the starboard side. They didn't seem to even know we were there. I could only see their backs and hear the "whoosh" as they exhaled. I could smell the fishy smell even at that distance.

The wind died as we got into the Yucatán Channel, so we started the engine. I wanted TIGGER to keep moving. I had called my daughter through the AT&T high seas operator, and my family had a big party planned for us the next weekend. We had lots of time to make it unless both the wind and the motor died. We both knew better than to tie ourselves to a schedule. But as long as there was wind for our sails and fuel in the tank, we would make a great effort to be there.

Now we were in the Gulf of Mexico, and there were ships all around us. We'd see about 20 ships a day, sometimes five or six at a time. But there were no close encounters. I had been a bit concerned about the Gulf. Early hurricanes sometimes form there. But the weather was very benign, with smooth seas, and dazzling, radiantly sunny days. No wind though, so we kept the engine humming until we couldn't stand the sound. Then we would drift for awhile. Two days from landfall, the wind came up from the southeast. We were sailing again, dodging oil rigs and shrimp boats, which insisted on dashing about in front and behind us, while I took our last days at sea into my heart to last for the upcoming year.

Hundreds of oil rigs litter the waters on the approach to Galveston. Looking at the chart, it seemed they would be difficult to miss, when actually they're many miles apart. For some reason TIGGER liked to play chicken with them, and the wind steering would inevitably head us right toward a rig. I knew when I saw a rig miles off, that I would have to pay attention until we had left it behind us. At night, the rigs were lit up like Las Vegas casinos. Sometimes we could see 18 or 20 of them on our horizon.

We crossed our outbound track a mere 40 miles from the outer sea buoy at the entrance to Galveston Bay. Then we docked at the Galveston Yacht Club at 1 a.m., June 4, 1998, four years and six months after we'd departed from the same spot. It was yet another night entrance, but this one we knew, and as we slowly motored through the humid night, I smiled and sighed. It was done, it was finished—the circle was complete.

The next day my son, Bill, and his sweetheart, Brenda, drove down from Houston to greet us and take us to lunch. And we spent the rest of the day resting and putting TIGGER right after 12 days at sea. The following day was blustery and cold. (In Houston? In June? Was this weather just for us?) Then we sailed 35 miles up the Houston Ship Channel, beating into the wind. The kids wanted us to enter the channel to Clear Lake at noon, so they could all be on the dock with their big banner welcoming us back. Naturally, we were an hour early, so we circled in the bay until it was time to make our grand entrance. It figures. We sail 35,000 miles without a schedule and here we are back in civilization, and we're early for our appointment!

The entrance channel is narrow and generally crowded with pleasure boats. But since the day was cool and cloudy, we had the place to ourselves. One side of the channel is lined with shrimp boats, mostly rusting and smelling like week-old shrimp. The other side is lined with trendy restaurants with decks where tourists sit and watch the boats go by.

Seagulls fly overhead, swooping and screaming, attracted by the week-old shrimp smell on one side and the fresh seafood smell on the other.

I had dreamed of coming home with all the flags of the countries we had visited flying on our backstay—all 24 of them—which is just what we did. And there was my treasured family, standing on the deck of one restaurant, their welcoming banner hung high for us to see. We waved and yelled hello and threw kisses while Dave maneuvered through the channel and got us safely to the marina. Then there were hugs and kisses for real, and laughter and everyone talking at once. That's how it's done in our family, everyone talking at once! That Sunday they had a big party at the marina clubhouse, and we were officially welcomed back by our family and friends.

Upon reflection, I'm not sure to what extent the trip changed me. I don't feel different, but I suspect I may be just a wee bit eccentric. I can't really claim I'm not a kook anymore. Just look at all the crazy things I did.

Most of all, I have filled my heart with longings and dreams at last realized. I have shared it all with the man I never thought I would find, and indeed, found in him a love that continues to grow and evolve. Before Dave, the world was tinted a different shade. It seems brighter now, more interesting and more hopeful. I have shown my children and grandchildren that you can dream big, no matter how crazy the dream may be. If it's yours, it's worthwhile, and just possibly, possible. At the same time, who am I kidding? This was for me, these were *my* lessons. Hey, did I just have a "coming of age" experience?

TIGGER, Dave and I are equal partners, and we each have our role. Dave is the captain (I let him be captain most of the time—do you think *I* want to be the one to get up at 3 a.m. to check the anchor?). TIGGER takes care of us, and I am the keeper of the stories. To me, that seems quite the way it should be.

So that's the story. At least the first part. The second part has yet to be written, either on paper or the tablet of our lives. There is still so much left to do, and so many places yet to see. You know, just beyond the horizon. The oceans are still there, waiting.

Other books of interest from Sheridan House

The Nathaniel Drinkwater Series

"Characters as rich as Patrick O'Brian's and as timeless as Forester's Hornblower."

An Eye of the Fleet: Drinkwater is part of a prize crew when initiative and courage enable him to survive a dangerous encounter.

A King's Cutter: Capt. Drinkwater is involved in secret and dangerous operations off the French Coast.

A Brig of War: Capt. Drinkwater is sent by Admiral Nelson to pursue his old enemy Edouard Santhonax during the French descent on India.

The Bomb Vessel: A young Capt. Drinkwater is given command of an old ship to be sent to the Baltic as a bomb vessel.

The Corvette: The splendor of the Arctic Ocean and the drama of a 19th century whale hunt unfold in this novel.

1805: Napoleon's powerful Combined Fleet is preparing to meet Admiral Nelson's British Fleet in the battle of Trafalgar.

Baltic Mission: Threatened by the discontent of his crew, Capt. Drinkwater is faced with the challenges brought about by military disaster and diplomatic intrigue.

In Distant Waters: Capt. Drinkwater is caught between Russian and Spanish enemies; his mission is made impossible by treachery.

A Private Revenge: Capt. Drinkwater brings His Britannic Majesty's frigate *Patrician* into the shelter of the Pearl River on the China coast.

Under False Colours: Capt. Drinkwater resolves on an exceptionally bold course of action—one not advised by the Admiralty.

The Flying Squadron: Capt. Drinkwater is ordered to the Chesapeake Bay in a last ditch effort to heal the rift between London and Washington.

Beneath The Aurora: While Napoleon faces defeat in Germany, Drinkwater gets caught up in the forbidding fjords of Norway.

The Shadow of the Eagle: Napoleon has abdicated and the 'Great War' is at an end, but Capt. Drinkwater receives secret intelligence of a new threat to peace.

Ebb Tide: During an inspection of lighthouses, tragedy strikes the aged and honorable Capt. Drinkwater. He is confronted with his past, his triumphs and disasters.

"This author has quietly stolen the weather gauge from most of his rivals in the Hornblower stakes."   —*OBSERVER*

America's Favorite Sailing Books
www.sheridanhouse.com

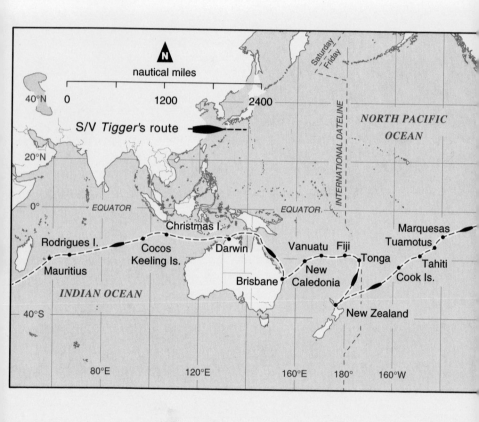